With What I Have Left

WITH WHAT I HAVE LEFT

MELISSA A. JAMES
WITH JO TUSCANO

Jo Tuscano is the author of the novel *The River Child* (Odyssey Books), co-author of *Back on the Block: Bill Simon's Story* (ASP/AIATSIS), and author of *This is Where You Have to Go* (Pantera Press). Jo works as a content creator for imagineer.me in cross-cultural education.

First published in 2024 by New Holland Publishers
Sydney

Level 1, 178 Fox Valley Road, Wahroonga, NSW 2076, Australia

newhollandpublishers.com

Copyright © 2024 New Holland Publishers
Copyright © 2024 in text: Melissa A. James

All rights reserved. No part of this publication may be reproduced, stored in a retrieval system or transmitted, in any form or by any means, electronic, mechanical, photocopying, recording or otherwise, without the prior written permission of the publishers and copyright holders.

A record of this book is held at the National Library of Australia.

ISBN 9781760796686

Managing Director: Fiona Schultz
Project Editor: Xavier Waterkeyn
Cover photograph: Andy Mayne Photography
Designer: Andrew Davies
Production Director: Arlene Gippert
Printed in China

10 9 8 7 6 5 4 3 2 1

Keep up with New Holland Publishers:

NewHollandPublishers

@newhollandpublishers

Contents

1. The Girl I Used to Be	7
2. The Spider	9
3. My Family	12
4. Fruit Loop	21
5. Going Places	35
6. Whose Wedding?	51
7. An Inconvenient Truth	62
8. Holey Plum	73
9. Square Metres	85
10. Mea Culpa	98
11. Hurt Me	112
12. The Karen Cult	124
13. Sea Change	138
14. Bucket List	156
15. Teapot and Sympathy	168
16. The Time of My Life	186

1. **The Girl I Used to Be**

My immediate hatred for her surprised me.

She walked up and stood near me, both of us waiting for the elevator. I was having a bad day. She was me, and she was not me. She was what I used to be. Tears formed, and I kept them back. I took in everything; her black heels, her legs that screamed sport, gym, exercise. Her tailored suit, crisp white shirt. The hair, perfectly straight. Light make-up. The leather bag, laptop size. She took out her mobile, spoke to someone about meeting targets and hung up. The elevator arrived. She motioned for me to enter first; of course, she would. She gave me a wan smile. I almost cried in front of her.

I walked into the elevator and didn't look at the mirrored walls. I didn't want to see me as I was; walking stick, flat, sensible shoes, hair tied back in a ponytail, comfortable, practical no-buttons-or-hook clothes, gait off centre – perhaps she thought I was drunk – bags under the eyes, dowdy, invisible to men. If I were on Tinder, you'd swipe left. She didn't see the cuts and scars I was so proud of, hidden under long sleeves. She didn't know the beautiful pain I craved. I was grateful she didn't speak to me. That morning, I was slurring my words. She alighted, and I heard her heels making click-click noises as she walked out. I stood, paralysed with grief, mourning my old life, the life she had now, a high flying corporate.

I wanted to go backwards, to morph into her. I didn't want to be me, dying. I didn't ask for this disease, this reduction of a life that had taken everything I had. The stage of acceptance that people talk about seemed a lifetime away if I lived that long. I stepped out of the elevator onto the floor that housed the medical specialists. Why me? I kept asking. Why me? The day before, I'd just come out of psychiatric care after yet another suicide attempt. My mother had organised for me to be in care for a while. I didn't want to go. Pumped with drugs, groggy and tired, I signed some papers. I remember my mother saying, "Just sign it, sweetie," I remember her saying, "You're a whore. You'll never amount to anything."

As I walked down the corridor, I saw her again, the girl that used to be me. She walked with purpose. I looked at her again before entering the door of the specialist. She was my old life, and I had to let it go. I didn't know how to do it, but I knew I had to do something, anything with the time I had left.

2. **The Spider**

I got through the ordeal by keeping my eyes on a spider. While the man grunted away, I watched the spider spinning its web, its perfectly patterned home taking shape, bit by bit. Methodical, purposeful, the spider knew exactly what it was doing. And here I was having sex for money in a toilet block, the floor littered with wet toilet paper, cigarette butts and used condoms. The stench of urine hit my nostrils. I read the graffiti on the cubicle walls. *For a good time, ring Sonia. Kim is a slut.* The windows above the cubicle were streaked with grime. I was streaked with grime on the inside, silently screaming. Hurry up. Hurry up.

Please, just finish.

He finished. We left the toilet block and drove straight to the bank. He gave me five thousand dollars. On the way back to the psychiatric hospital, neither of us spoke. I couldn't wait to have a shower. I told him I couldn't stay and talk. He told me he had to go home to his wife and kids.

He was supposed to have been a friend. It was 2008, and I had been admitted to Mosman Private's psychiatric ward. I was there from February to April. While I was recovering, I was stressed about finances as I was running out of money. The hospital fees were not cheap. I didn't know how I was going to survive. I had to find somewhere to live and pay rent. I needed money for food, bills, medicine, doctors and specialists and health fund payments. My credit card was almost maxed out. My disability pension had not yet come through. The only option was a homeless shelter, refuge, hospital or live in my car. This situation was a constant source of stress, and I couldn't stop thinking about it. It plagued me day and night. The loop tape went round and round in my head.

Get discharged. Find job.

Have money. Find place to live.

The staff were told that no calls from my family were to be put through to me as they would verbally attack me. One afternoon, however, a nurse put through a call from my father.

"When are you going to get your act together?" he asked. "You need to take responsibility for your situation."

The nurse was reprimanded for letting that call go through. I couldn't stop thinking about what my father had said. He didn't understand how a person couldn't just snap out of major depression and get on with it. How was I supposed to get my act together? What was my act anyway? What wasn't I taking responsibility for? I knew I was responsible for everything that went wrong. I had always been told that, and I believed it. So, wasn't that taking responsibility? On the day I accepted money for sex, I had been allowed out on day release.

The 'old friend' had come to visit me one morning. He was a very wealthy man. This man had wanted to have a relationship with me, and I had always said no. I wasn't attracted to him romantically or sexually, but that wasn't the only reason. He was married and had three children. I was very anxious on the morning he visited. I was mulling over my financial situation and ended up confiding in him about how broke I was.

"I'll give you five thousand dollars," he said. "It's not a loan. You don't have to pay me back, but there is one thing I ask in return."

He turned to face me. By then, we were walking through a park. "I want us to have sex. Just once."

I stood there, speechless. The idea was repugnant to me, but as I was standing there, I heard my father's voice in my head. *Take responsibility. Take responsibility.* I decided that perhaps this was a way of taking responsibility for getting out of debt. Yes, I decided as my future flashed before my eyes – no more debt. Credit card paid off without accruing more interest. Enough for a bond to get a place. No more sleeping in my car. Rent paid while I looked for work. Enough money to eat properly. This was called taking responsibility.

"All right," I said.

He could hear the reluctance in my voice. "Where?"

"There," he said, motioning toward the toilet block. "No way," I said. "Absolutely not."

"You'll change your mind if we don't do it soon."

He was right about that.

Back at the hospital, under the shower, I scrubbed furiously, hurting myself.

Disgusting.

You're disgusting, I told myself. To have stooped so low as to have sex with a guy for money in a public toilet made me feel sick. I judged myself harshly; it took the shine out of being debt-free. I felt depressed and filthy. I didn't feel like I'd taken responsibility. I scrubbed till my skin was red and sore. I felt like I wanted to end it all.

I promised myself that I would never do that ever again. That incident made me realise that I couldn't judge sex workers for doing what they did. Desperation makes people do things that they usually wouldn't do. There was a time I considered being an escort but with no sex, the type that businessmen want when they need a partner at a function, but the idea faded as my body slowly broke down. Much later, when I was able to process events in my life with some help, I was filled with anger at that man. He took advantage of a mentally ill patient in a psychiatric hospital. Yes, I was a consenting adult, but I was a consenting adult who was not in a fit mental state to make decisions about anything. He was a selfish opportunist with no morals. I was so afraid of people finding out, fearful of people judging me and seeing me as a certain type of person, that I told nobody. I kept the dirty sex-in-the-toilet-block-for-money secret to myself for a long time. Much later, I understood that the incident in the toilet block didn't define who I was. I was at one of the lowest points in my life, and that man, who should have known better, had preyed on me.

After I was discharged from Mosman, I went straight to the tattooist and got some more ink on my body. I needed to feel pain. It didn't help. I wanted the needle to go so deep that it would pierce through my heart. The pain level wasn't strong enough to wash away the abhorrence I felt about what I had done. I lay in bed that night and thought about my life, about its beginnings, its journey, and about how it had come to this. I tried to find reasons, a pattern, answers to questions I still had, anything that would let me understand why my life had turned out as it had. None of it made sense.

3. My Family

I grew up in a house, not a home.

At the time of my birth in 1975, my family lived in a beautiful old federation house with traditional mouldings, and a fireplace, all the way down to the original green bathtub. The kitchen cupboards were wooden. Mum got sick of asking Dad to update the kitchen, so she laminated all the insides of the cupboards. When she opened them, at least she saw something new. She felt at least something had been changed.

The house was always spotless; nothing was ever out of place. When my parents' first grandchild came along, people said, "Soon, you will have to move everything up high."

Mum said no, "She will learn as my children did, look, but not touch." I believe I was the only one who broke something. I started walking at nine months. Actually, I just got up and ran. No crawling, just got up and started running. I didn't know how to stop running and broke a black clock cat in the hallway. I learnt there was, of course, no running allowed. No running, no touching and that was the hard part – there was stuff everywhere. Mum had decorated every corner of the house; it was nicely done but entirely over the top in a sort of Maltese-Aussie kitsch sort of way. Every door had a gold tassel hanging from it. All the windows had bars, not to keep us in but to keep intruders out – a total fire hazard.

One Christmas, my mother hung strands of fairy lights off every tree in the garden. Our house looked like a magical wonderland, ablaze with twinkling stars. We lived not too far from the airport. A friend once said, "My God, it's a wonder the planes don't get mixed up when landing." After that Christmas, my father went to take the lights down. My mother urged him to leave them up for just a little while longer. A little while longer tuned into a lot longer so that my father didn't ever get to take them down. They remained a permanent fixture, so much so that nobody ever had to give too many directions on how to find our house.

I remember wishing the magical feeling permeating the garden would seep into the house and do some good there, but I was disappointed.

We were nominal Catholics, attending mass at Easter and Christmas. I attended a Catholic school for my primary and secondary schooling. I was a believer, but only because we were told that we had to; there was no other choice. Doin' the Catholic thing. The nuns were strict, and we had to do Religious Studies as part of the curriculum.

Our house was split-level. The family was split level. The kitchen, bathroom, my parents' room, my brother's room, the TV room, dining room, sitting room, ironing room and what became my bedroom were on the main level. The living room accommodated the stairs up to the attic, which became the computer room and my eldest sister's bedroom. The stairs led down to the study and Dad's workroom, which then led out to the downstairs shower, bathroom, and laundry room. Off the kitchen were the back stairs leading to the back yard and rumpus room.

Many times, these stairs made an excellent escape route. If I was in trouble, about to be smacked and making a run for it, the house provided great opportunities with all its levels and stairs. And I was in trouble from an early age.

"You're useless," my mother told me. "You'll never amount to much," she said.

My father never said I was useless, but his patriarchal Maltese upbringing cemented the old beliefs that girls weren't quite as valuable as boys.

If I was in trouble, I could run down the stairs from the living room through Dad's workroom, through the bathroom and into the yard, allowing for an easy getaway – just as long as the bathroom door wasn't locked and the person pursuing you hadn't outsmarted you by taking the stairs off the kitchen to the back yard and waiting on the other side of the bathroom door. When Dad renovated the house, I had a room of my own.

I loved being alone. I felt at peace. Four walls, the door closed, silence. Mine. All mine. Nobody else existed. I could do what I wanted and have the room exactly as I wanted. I loved the smell of clean and tidy. Nothing was ever going to be out of place. I could coordinate everything without being laughed at. No one could barge in whenever they wanted; no lights were going on and off at all hours, and no one ran past making noise. I didn't have to change in the bathroom. I was good at gymnastics, so I stretched a lot. I also sang as loud as I wanted to. I could read as much as I wanted without interruption or funny looks. No one in my family read. I didn't have to listen to others' conversations and wait for my turn to speak. I didn't have to listen to what was being analysed or discussed. I didn't have to listen to comments about how useless I was. It was my haven away from my mother's constant criticism and her comments about everything I said or did. It was here that I began to have conversations with the other me.

"You're not useless, you know, Melissa," I said. "Yes, I know. I know."

"Why does she say I'm useless?"

"I don't know. I don't know what I've done wrong. Nothing I do ever pleases her."

"Don't worry. Just keep going."

"But it's hard because isn't Mum always right?"

My room was the one place where quiet existed. I was myself. I read, I wrote in my journal, and I let my imagination run wild. I would only come out when called. Dad would always say, 'Leave your door open' or 'What are you hiding in there?' Even later, as a teenager, I wasn't loud. I didn't date or go to clubs. I didn't take drugs or sleep with boys. I was just plain me, quiet, conservative, alone. From an early age, I was sick, and illness plagued me through childhood and into my teenage years. I never thought about family until much later in my life and just accepted that we were just like most other families. The people who I thought were my grandparents were the only grandparents I'd known. They were a strong and positive presence in my life.

My maternal grandmother was 'Nanny', and my maternal grandfather was 'Grandad.' Nanny was of the blue rinse era. Going to the city was called going to 'town', and of course, you wore your best dress, gloves, hat, pantyhose, polished closed-in shoes and your face was always made up perfectly. Mills and Boon books were her favourites. Nan was always home. Many women didn't work back then. I can still see her sitting at the kitchen bench reading, always reading, same seat, same position.

Grandad was the complete opposite. Back in the day, both Nan and Grandad were from Orange in Sydney, New South Wales. Grandad would sell fruit and vegetables door to door. He was an entrepreneur from the start. When they moved to Sydney, they lived in Glebe. They bought boarding houses and also managed them for someone else. This involved long hours of emotional and physical labour. Grandad had very thick skin. Eventually, they owned many properties in Glebe, but of course, that didn't stop Grandad. Between Grandad going to war and Nanny enduring many miscarriages, they started a family-owned and run business.

Grandad was very wealthy, but he always wore singlets with holes in them and pants with braces. Brylcreem was always a morning ritual, as was cooking bubble 'n' squeak.

I spent a lot of time with Grandad doing deliveries and driving all over the place. Grandad believed it was saving the company money. Grandad's company employed the kids in my family. We put nuts and bolts together to make skateboards. We were paid $5.00 per box. We then had to place them in separate bags. The boxes contained at least two thousand pieces each. It was tedious work.

I never met my biological grandparents; the only picture of my biological grandmother is her height. She stood at five foot nine. I found out at nineteen that my 'grandparents' were Mum's aunt and uncle.

They had one child, a son. Mum's mother died when she was twelve, and she was raised by a relative and her father. Even so, Mum basically raised herself and her younger brother. Mum's father was an alcoholic. He earned a good salary, but he would always drink it away. My biological grandmother died from cancer, but I'm sure that years of physical and psychological abuse from her husband played a huge role. Her husband was six feet tall and strong. He would bash my mother mostly because she was a girl, and he only wanted boys.

"You're no good coz you're only a girl," he would tell her. "You're not wanted." Often, my mother's and her brother's nightly meal was a packet of chips from a vending machine and a soft drink at the Campsie pub. They would sit out in the gutter, waiting for my grandmother to come out of the side door of the pub and quickly throw them their food before going back inside again. My grandmother had no choice in this situation. She either went to the pub with her husband and did precisely what he told her to do or else suffered a brutal beating. These were not the days when a woman with no means of support and two children could easily leave her husband. She didn't have the resources to find out about the welfare system and accommodation. She had nobody to turn to for help. Added to this was the shame of her situation in those times. She felt she didn't have options.

Mum developed ways of surviving. She became a tomboy and often got into fights defending her young brother. She was tall, skinny, and tough. She could run and run fast. After many years of physical and mental abuse, my mother and her brother ran from the house, never to return. My grandfather was very drunk, and a neighbour from across the street advised my mother and her brother not to go into the house and instead run to a relative's house. They ran to the house of an aunt and uncle, and this is where they stayed permanently. She was fourteen, and her brother was ten.

I always thought that with her background, Mum might have gone the other way, and I was always so proud of how she chose to be better and not let her past dictate her future. I now understand because of her aunt and uncle, whom she came to call Mum and Dad, she was given a fantastic opportunity. She was fourteen when she went to live with my grandparents. She worked hard in the boarding houses. She often spoke of the manual labour and the long hours. Grandad believed in hard work, and I am sure this is where she developed her work ethic and respect for herself, understanding and respecting others. I realised how much courage and willingness my Mum showed at the age of fourteen. When she met my Dad, she was a trainee hairdresser. She never finished her course. I had no idea that her dysfunctional upbringing was to have an impact on me.

At age nineteen, I processed all this information with the maturity that any nineteen-year-old had and moved on. As a teenager, my grandparents living across the road from us wasn't always ideal. My parents often suggested that I go and visit my grandparents, and I would groan and complain, asking my parents why I had to visit them over the road when they were always at our house anyway. My nanny would sit in the same chair in our kitchen, waiting for us to walk in and kiss her. She had a habit of leaning forward, tucking our hair behind our ears, and saying, 'Sweetheart, let me see your face. You have such a beautiful face. Don't hide it.' As I matured, these memories are the things I cherish. Even now, I find myself tucking my hair behind my ears, and every time I do, I think of my nanny. I wouldn't have wanted different grandparents for anything in the world.

I never met my paternal grandmother, Dana, as she died before I was born.

Dad was one of six, born in Malta. When I was a small child, I thought Dad was quite exotic as he wasn't born in Australia. I had heard stories about the stalk bringing babies and imagined something better for my father. In my imagination, he was born in a cabbage. There was a field of cabbages, but my father's cabbage was the best and most prominent of them all. I heard many years later that Dad's mother disapproved of my mother.

"Have some fun with her, but don't marry her," she had said.

Nanna Dana frowned on the very short skirts that my mother used to wear. On one occasion, she told my mother off.

"Keep your legs closed. You're not showing us anything new," she said.

Dad's father, Nanu, was an imposing man. Short, dark, and surly, we lived in fear of him. A hard man, his idea of fixing his dental problems was to tie a piece of string to his tooth, tie the other end to a door handle, and pull. My brother hated visiting him as Nanu would pinch his cheeks so hard that my brother would be in pain for a few days. Every two weeks, on the journey in our family van, my brother would dread the visit. When we pulled up outside Nanu's house, my father would turn off the ignition and turn around in his seat. He'd sigh. That sigh filled us with foreboding. We knew what was coming.

"You will be seen but not heard."

Anything to do with Nanu was done with military precision. Like the Von Trapps, we lined up in order of age, the oldest being the first to kiss him and say hello. His idea of a cuddle, if the children tried to do that, was to pat them on the back. We learned to read Dad's face for approval for the simplest things, like going to the toilet and asking for a glass of water. We had to read Dad's face to gauge whether we were doing the right thing in Nanu's house. If Nanu offered us anything like chocolate, we had to take it for fear of offending him. We would look at Dad for approval. Nanu never offered us a drink, ever. His second wife, Lilly, whom we called Nanna Lilly, would offer us a drink, and we would look at Dad for permission. We knew just by looking at his eyes and the slight nod of his head that the answer had to be "no".

Dad was the product of the migrant experience: strict, austere, and mindful of never wasting money. He had a habit of never being fully engaged in watching television. He would always have his head slightly bent away, never looking straight ahead at the screen, with one eye averted as to whatever else was going on in the house. The children in Nanu's house sat in age order while watching television. Dad used to tell us that being the fourth born, he sat further to the back and got used to watching television, craning his head to see through the spaces of bodies in front of him. He arrived in Australia with his immediate family when he was one year old. In the early days, he was the spitting image of Jerry Lewis. But over the years, he has become more of a chocolate box, a mix of Robert De Niro, and a splash of Denzel Washington, all wrapped up with the height of Robin Williams. His family disapproved of him marrying an Australian woman. They wanted him to marry a Maltese. I once asked him, "Why am I so short compared to my brother, who is six feet tall, and my sisters, who are average height?"

He just looked at me and said, "I was very tired that night, sorry."

He was the archetypal Maltese immigrant. When he went shopping or buying anything through a private sale, he bargained his way to the cheapest price by asking, 'How much for cash?' It didn't matter if it was a lot of money involved and he didn't have it on him at the time. It didn't matter whether it was a small item or a car.

"I'll be back later," he'd say. "With cash."

When my siblings and I were old enough to understand the value of water views, we told Dad we'd love to have one.

"There's a fishpond in our front yard," he said. "There's water in it. That's a water view."

As far as the yard went, Dad would have concreted over everything if he'd had his way.

We didn't see much of Dad when we were growing up. He worked all the time and was not very involved in our day to day lives. We only saw him for about an hour a day. He would eat dinner in front of the TV, then shower and be off the bed. He would be gone in the morning before sunrise. He had several jobs. Sometimes, he would not come home as a Sunday rolled into a Monday, which he would call a Smonday. As soon as Dad got home, we would all run to our desks and make it look like we had been there since we got home from school. My mother would shout out to us, "Quick, your father's home. Hurry up and look like you're studying." Her tone of voice and facial expression told us my father was a man to be feared.

We were always waiting for the smack, for not sitting right, not trying hard enough. Anything and everything equalled a smack. If my mother wanted us to be afraid of him, she succeeded. My father was typical of many migrants who expected great things from their children as they had come to a new country to give their kids the opportunities they missed. When I did well on an exam or essay, I couldn't wait to show my father. I wanted to make him proud. If I got ninety-eight per cent, he would say, "What did you do wrong?" or "Where are the other two per cent?"

According to my mother, the other two per cent went missing because I was a failure.

"You'll never amount to anything," she said. "It's a wonder you even got that mark."

I quickly stopped sharing or being proud of my achievements. Sometimes, my father could be fun, especially when we were little. He would play-bite, telling me that arm or foot or toe belonged to him, and he wanted it back. I would scream with laughter. I can look back and thank him for helping me become who I am today. With my very bumpy journey, having a thick and determined skin has served me well. He was tough. It made me tough, as well.

As I got older, I realised that his strict way of child-rearing was because he just wanted his children to be brought up the right way. He knew only the way that Nanu and Nanna, his mother, had raised him. He taught me many excellent qualities, morals, and values I will use for the rest of my life. He taught me right from wrong. My parents had very different attitudes to money. Because of Dad's upbringing, he was tight with money, and he drilled it into our heads to save for the things we wanted. Like many migrants who had come from nothing, he hated waste. For every ten dollars we saved as kids, Dad would match it with another ten. He had seen his relatives buy cars for their children and believed that those children learned nothing about saving. My mother was the opposite. Put it on credit and think about it later, she told us.

I can't pin down the time when my Mum went from being Mum to just my mother. Once she was Mum. We spent nine long months together, it being a complicated pregnancy. I wanted to come three months early, and, in those days, they put women on alcoholic drips to stop labour. In the delivery room, I was coming out with one hand over my head; I was inquisitive even then. I wanted to touch and feel before I was sure I wanted to enter. Because of the difficult delivery, which could have resulted in both mother and child dying, I spent the first three months of my life in hospital. Apparently, I was the perfect child, falling into a routine straight away. Mum had four kids under five, so I suppose she was glad the new baby didn't present too much of a challenge.

"It almost killed me, her delivery. I could've died."

I was to hear this story many times in my life. It meant nothing to me as a child, but later, it took on different shades of meaning. Guilt began to creep into my psyche. I almost killed her; it was up to me to please her and make her happy.

I had grommets put in my ears when I was two years old, and not long after, my tonsils and adenoids were removed. I learned I had glue ear, and the grommets, over time, would fall out. No one noticed I was deaf until Mum started wondering why I wouldn't respond when she was talking directly to me, and then when I had my back to her, I wouldn't respond at all. To me, she wasn't even there. I got a lot of smacks for not listening. I didn't understand why I was suddenly hit. A specialist finally worked it out. One day at school, when I was in second grade, a small, clear, round apparatus with wires inside fell out of my right ear. I was terrified and began to panic. My Mum was called to try and calm me down. I wondered whether I was human or perhaps an alien. My head was coming out through my ears. I was made of wires and bits. No one explained what was happening and why.

I often heard my mother on the phone to her friends, complaining about me. "She's always sick. And now she has to have her tonsils out. I'm exhausted with this child. What have I done to deserve this?"

My siblings picked up on my mother's resentment. Her web of lies about me was spun early, and they believed her. Because I was so often sick, I developed an idea from a young age that I was a burden on my mother, and as an extension of this idea, I also believed that I deserved pain because I was such a problem child. Even though pain hurt physically, something about being in pain brought some relief. I believed I needed to suffer to make up for all the disruption I was causing my family. It was the counterbalance to all the problems that I caused for my parents. It was the start of self-harm. Every time I made her upset, I had to hurt myself. I hurt myself a lot.

4. Fruit Loop

Despite having four small children, Mum kept our house spotless. Mum had one room in the house, the ironing room, that was allowed to be messy, and it was. All those loads of washing, ironing. I am sure she threw everything in there and just closed the door. One day, I followed her in when I was two years old, and as my vocabulary was limited, all I said was, "Clean up, clean up." Mum said she was dumbfounded as she watched me pick up things and put them on the floor at her feet. It was simply learned behaviour. I watched her; I copied her. "Clean up, clean up" were two of my first words.

I showed an ability for athletics and gymnastics from an early age and started doing gymnastics at four. My sisters were indoor types, on the phone, watching TV, or trying on different outfits, whereas I loved being outdoors. I spent my time in shorts and a tee-shirt, getting dirty, climbing trees, riding my skateboard or BMX bike. I never liked make-up and still don't. My brother and I became inseparable. When I wasn't outside, I was in my room, never wanting to leave my surroundings. That always got me in a lot of trouble. My parents would shout as I was always behind closed doors. I had friends at school, but I knew never to invite them home. Nobody ever told me I couldn't ask my classmates home, but instinct told me it wouldn't be allowed. Therefore, I didn't get a chance to see how other families behaved and what roles in the family looked like.

Mum enrolled all four kids at the local Youth Club, where we undertook tap, ballet, and gymnastics. My sisters preferred tap and ballet with their tutus, hair spray, and spangled tops. Too prissy for me, I preferred the rumble and tumble of gymnastics. I had a coach who saw something in me. I had a go at everything and would not stop until I succeeded. The desire to succeed at all costs, inherited from my father, was ingrained in me.

"See, you can be good at something!" my inner voice said. "But keep it to yourself. Don't get too proud."

"I'm not telling anyone. I don't want to get into trouble."

Most afternoons, Mum would take me to gymnastics. She would wait with the other mothers. This meant Andrew had to come. Andrew, like all toddlers, could not be still. Andrew was a very determined and inquisitive youngster. One afternoon, when Mum was distracted, he decided he would put his head through the gap between the top and bottom of a chair, and he couldn't get it out.

The fire brigade arrived and quickly assessed the situation. Sawing the chair was not an option; it was dangerous, as toddlers squirm when they are panicking. The only option was a slow and tedious one. They had to unscrew every bolt on the chair. Finally, after a good twenty minutes, Andrew was free. He was free from the chair, but after that, he was not free from Mum when we went to gymnastics. Mum tied him to a chair and didn't let him move. I begged Mum not to bring Andrew, but after the chair incident, he was always tied up as soon as we entered the gym, and he didn't dare speak a word.

On another occasion, when Andrew disagreed with Mum, he packed his bag and his favourite toy, Froggy, and decided to run away. Mum caught up with him and asked why he was waiting at the corner.

"I'm not allowed to cross the road by myself," he replied. "And Froggy wants a drink, thank you."

Because my sisters and I were so different, they perceived I was too young to hang around with them. I found that quite devastating. I soldiered on with my 'tomboy' activities, which I loved. I had a BMX bike, a skateboard, roller skates, rollerblades, ice skates, a baseball bat, gloves, and other sporting equipment. I spent my time learning how to jump stairs, ride down steps, climb trees, and ride my skateboard down the street so fast that I sometimes didn't know how to stop. After some serious accidents, I learned quickly.

Despite being a tomboy, I had some dolls. One day, my sisters decided they wanted to have a doll wedding. They took one of my dolls, cutting the hair off to make it a boy. Again, I was devastated. They thought it was funny. They thought I should act more like a girl.

When I was twelve, I experienced a strange phenomenon one night. My legs became so sore and weak that I couldn't walk, so I slithered on my belly and used my arms to propel myself up the hallway to the bathroom and back to my bedroom. I didn't tell anyone, and it didn't happen again, but it left me bewildered.

"Melissa, why are you crawling like a snake up the hallway?" asked the other me.

"I don't know. I can't use my legs tonight."

"Well, let's not worry about it. For now."

I put it to the back of my mind and got on with life. The incident with the legs was a one-off, and it didn't stop me from climbing into the top cupboards in our house. Because I was a gymnast, I did this easily. Dad knew I sometimes hid in the top cupboards, but he never let on, even when Mum called out my name. He told her he didn't know where I was.

Despite being two years younger, Andrew was stronger than me and could sometimes be quite mean to me. One of his favourite jokes was to tie me to a low chair and put it behind two large recliner chairs in the loungeroom, which he pushed together. When Mum came home, the first thing she noticed was the chairs in the wrong place. She found me tied up, but Andrew was never punished. I didn't think this was fair, and one afternoon, I got my own back on my brother.

Andrew had his head in the freezer one afternoon and was licking the ice (I don't know why) when his tongue got stuck on the frozen surface. He tried to pull it off but couldn't, as it hurt too much. I boiled the jug and poured it over the frozen tongue. Andrew screamed and spluttered. Pink skin fell on the floor, a layer of tongue in a shrivelled mess. He gave me a filthy look, and when he tried to speak, I couldn't understand him. He kept very quiet for the next few days so my parents wouldn't notice, but his meanness stopped toward me. Mum commented on his strange speech, but he didn't dob me in. At the time, I knew what I did was terrible, but I was so sick of Mum not punishing him that I needed to teach him a lesson.

"Melissa," said the other me, "that was really cruel. Why did you do that?"

"Why doesn't mum punish him when he's mean to me? Why? It's not fair."

"I can't answer that."

Strangely enough, Andrew and I got on better after that.

My brother and I spent years together until I hit high school. Things then were different. My sisters saw me differently again. I became Tegan's shadow. I was now seen as cute and not so annoying. Things were constantly changing. I was becoming a woman with all the changes that take place – mood swings, attitude, frustrations. At this point, in high school, I started withdrawing. Being born hearing impaired creates a certain kind of isolation, and not being able to sometimes recognise your mother's voice is confusing.

My father was very good at mathematics. I was quite good at maths, and my father always wanted to know what was happening in maths class. I was in Year Seven. I was scared of my father when we had to sit down together and look at a maths problem. It didn't matter if I got the answer right or wrong; I was fearful of getting it wrong after he had explained it, hoping that I'd understand his explanation. I was terrified of not getting it right, as well. Just thinking about answering was so scary, so I froze. I could tell he was getting frustrated because he was biting his knuckles. It's a Maltese thing. One night, he got angry when he asked me what the answer to a long division problem was. I simply didn't know. He took off his thong, a big thong with lots of padding on the bottom. He whacked it across my face. Shocked, I stayed still, my skin burning. If I had cried, he would have done it again. His attitude to emotions was the old-fashioned Maltese way: you don't show emotions. Emotional people were weak. My mother, who had walked into the room and had seen the whacking, said nothing to my father.

"Melissa, time for bed," was all she said.

My first real paying job came at fourteen and six months. In those days, you legally weren't allowed to work until you were fourteen and nine months old, but I just couldn't wait. I got a casual job at the local fruit shop on Thursday nights and Saturdays. I loved it. I learnt to stock the shelves, refresh packs, and gain knowledge about different fruits and vegetables and their seasons. I learned to run the checkout as well. Then came the day when my eating disorder began.

In 1989, when I was fourteen, the girls in our year were put through a 'fat test' by the physical education teachers in our school. A fat test involves pinching back fat with calipers to measure the amount of body fat a person carries. The test was done in front of everyone, and therefore, there was competition about the results between the girls, setting off psychological stress in me regarding body issues and weight. I don't know if this test is still done in schools, and I hope it isn't because I believe it is a dangerous thing to do with young girls who are vulnerable to media messages and the comments of other girls. I know some states in the USA have outlawed fat tests in schools because of the mental health problems it causes. The fat test really messed with my head, and for the next year, I was obsessed with what went into my mouth. The fat test was the worst thing for a girl like me; it had a lot to do with my problems in the future in terms of my relationship with food.

By 1991, at sixteen years of age, I had anorexia but didn't want to admit it. I had always had stomach problems and spent a lot of my time when I did eat on the toilet. Mum took me to doctors to find out what was wrong, but the doctors decided I just wanted attention and dismissed my illness as a psychological cry for attention. They then prescribed anti-depressants. I became even more depressed. I didn't know what was wrong, but I knew it wasn't about attention. I spent years with my stomach problem without proper medical help. Anti-depressants were the doctors' answer to everything. My eating disorder was never discussed at home, as my parents believed that doctors were always right in their diagnosis of attention-seeking. My mother moaned to her friends on the phone.

"Now she has stomach problems! Can you believe it? I spend all my time running around to doctors only to be told it's all in her head and she needs a shrink, for God's sake! I'm so tired."

"Poor Karen," her friends said. "What a burden!"

The stomach problem caused a lot of stress during dinner time.

"We aren't leaving this table until you finish everything on your plate."

This was a common mantra in our house. It often took till 11.00 pm for my Dad to give up and tell me to get to bed. Over the years, I learned how to get through a meal without eating what was put in front of me. Mum would always cook peas, and I hated them. I still do. Putting the peas in my mouth, I would take a drink, and with one swig, I would swallow every pea without chewing. I started doing it with all my food. Mum was not a good cook, and I didn't like the way she cooked most things. As we got older, it was easy to trick Mum as we were always coming and going, and our friends would come over, extended family would turn up, and it was easier for my rituals to go undetected. Mum didn't have a chance of keeping an eye on me; there really were too many of us.

Food and I have never been friends. I didn't have time for it, and it didn't interest me, it hurt to eat, and when I ate, I would be on the toilet for days. Food equalled pain. Mum suffered from a disease called Celiac. She would tell me:

"We eat to survive, not to enjoy."

I was tested for the same disease, and my brother and sisters were as well. I came back as gluten intolerant, meaning my stomach was only able to tolerate a small amount of gluten or wheat products before it started hurting again. The 'we eat to live, not to enjoy' was always playing in my head. Despite my eating disorder, I had always been good at sports and was interested in food and health. I read about nutrition and told my family what I had found out.

'That's rubbish,' my mother would say.

However, if anyone else told her the same information, she would take it on board.

By now, my parents had me in the "too-hard basket." They didn't understand what I was going through. When I watched television, I saw how families in television land encouraged their children. When their children were sick, they were caring and kind. They put them to bed and brought in ice cream and hot drinks. They asked questions. "Does it still hurt? Are you feeling better? Mummy will sit here until you fall asleep." They told them they could do anything if they put their minds to it or worked hard. Work hard, and the rest will follow. My experience was not like that.

"You're a failure," my mother would tell relatives in front of me. "She's a fruit loop." My favourite was, "You won't amount to much, so I guess we will always have to take care of you forever." Another favourite was, "You have absolutely no common sense."

After a while, it became easy to believe because I was young, and they were my parents. I believed that parents were supposed to be right about everything. I never questioned any of the statements that my parents made about me. I learned to accept them, and years of accepting them led to believing these statements. The most dangerous lies are not the ones that others tell you; they're the ones you tell yourself. I was still talking to myself, but the other self was now less inclined to disagree.

"Will they always have to take care of me? Am I really that bad?"

"Maybe you are. You have to try harder."

In my family's eyes, I was the 'whole package.' All I had was sickness, and everyone had had enough. A day never went by without pain and suffering. I learned from a young age to keep my feelings and degree of pain to myself.

Mum could always see the pain; it showed in my eyes, and my face. I tried my best to hide it, but I knew she could see it. I was never asked about the pain or what degree of pain I was in, nor was I offered any medication to ease it. Because I was 'pretending' to be in pain to get 'attention,' it was treated as though it didn't exist.

"You have a shocking attitude," my mother said. "We all hate your attitude."

I took up a lot of Mum's time, and I am sure my siblings resented me for it. I can look back and understand. Jealously played a considerable role in the way my siblings treated me. I wanted to believe that Mum could see my pain but used tough love to make me tougher so I could get through it. As for my attitude, I didn't know I had one. I didn't understand what an attitude actually was. All I knew was that whatever I was doing was wrong, and everybody hated it. Dad always said, "Children are to be seen but not heard," so I didn't voice my bewilderment over this shocking attitude I had somehow acquired. I had no idea what it was or where it came from. Because my mother said negative things about me, my siblings caught on. Even though we didn't fight and generally got on quite well, they often called me a 'waste of space' and a 'fruit loop.'

Sometimes, at night, I'd lay awake and ponder about attitude. "What's an attitude?"

"I don't know. But all I know is that mine is bad."

"But what will happen to me if it's really bad?"

"I can't answer that. Just try to improve it, whatever it is."

One afternoon, I got stuck in the car with Mum when it broke down while I was on the way to a medical appointment. We had to wait for the NRMA. While waiting, my mother suddenly launched into a tirade about her childhood. She sounded angry and resentful.

"I was always in hospital – eleven hospitalisations in ten years. Yes, of course, everybody felt sorry for me, but what good is that? Everyone just has to make a choice to get on with it. Other people's lives go on, and yours doesn't. I just said to myself enough is enough. I'm done with this feeling sorry for myself, so I stopped."

I didn't understand this; it was as though people who were sick had a simple choice to 'get on with it.' It confused me. I didn't ask why she was hospitalised, and something told me not to ask. I thought a lot about it but only became more confused. I didn't want to be sick and didn't want to be in pain, but I couldn't make the illness go away, and I wasn't aware that I was feeling sorry for myself. I never complained, so how did she know I was feeling sorry for myself?

Once again, I had managed to upset her. I had to be punished for this. I found relief in hurting myself. I pinched myself. I punched myself. I cut myself. It had to be done.

One of the most memorable times growing up was when I was twelve and my sister got a weekend job at a nursing home. She needed a kitchen hand. I was only twelve, but I wanted that job. The oldies in the dining room never made it straight-forward.

"It was sunny when I made my decision, now I want to change it," or "This salad is cold," or "What was I thinking when I ordered this?" or "That looks better than mine."

I was always on the run, trying not to get behind and, at the same time, trying to keep them all happy. I was on my feet from the minute we got there to the minute we left.

I became very close to a few of the elderly people there. In retrospect, I realise it was a lot for a twelve-year-old. I would clean the kitchen as fast as I possibly could. I did this so I could go and help the nurses. I would clean the residents' teeth. Most had false teeth. No matter how old someone was, they wanted to keep their teeth in. I would have to wrestle with them sometimes to get their teeth out. They would suck them in, and nothing would make them budge. I would always check on everyone before we left to go home. It makes me laugh to think about the Occupational Health and Safety aspects of a twelve-year-old pulling out nursing home residents' teeth today!

One afternoon, while I was checking the rooms, I noticed something was wrong. The room was cold. I quietly moved around the room to check on everyone. The older woman in the last bed was dying. I had cleaned her teeth around half an hour earlier, and she was breathing normally. She had seemed all right. I grabbed hold of her hand and told her someone was with her and that it was all right to let go. I remember listening to her take her last breath. I called the nurses, and they took over. I can't believe the strength I had at that age. I was so grateful I was able to be with her so that she knew someone was there with her and that her last breath was taken with someone. She was not alone.

My sister and I kept working there until one of my 'favourites' passed away.

I thank God it was a day I wasn't there. My Mum had to tell me. It was getting harder and harder to watch them getting frailer and frailer. It was difficult not to love these beautiful, intelligent human beings who had so much to give and express. I was young and couldn't handle the fact that they were passing away. It was time to leave. Working at the nursing home taught me so many things: empathy, understanding, kindness, respect, and, most of all, the beauty of the elderly. It was hard to leave, but losing person after person was heartbreaking. I believe it is a job that every young person should do even for a few weeks as it teaches them so much, not only about respect for your elders but also respect for yourself. I became stronger because of my experiences there, and the wisdom that was passed on to me from the elderly people had an effect on me. It made me appreciate my grandparents a lot more as I got older. I would give anything to have spent more time with them as I believe they enriched my life.

My next casual job was at Target. I worked there throughout my high school years. I started at the check-out and later progressed to lay-by supervisor. I was good at my job, and I learned quickly.

Perhaps because I was growing up and on the verge of being a teenage girl, my relationship with my brother started to dwindle, and I started working and spending a lot more time with Tegan. Amanda was moving on and had outgrown hanging out with her little sister, so Tegan began to hang out with me, and in turn, I grew out of being a tomboy and grew out of hanging out with my little brother.

My hair had always been up because I was always outside doing activities that saw me get dirty. I liked to play in mud and do other things that might have been awkward with my hair down. Now, I started to wear my hair down. I stopped riding a skateboard and roller skates and spent less time outside. I also began to read. Nanny always read, and she encouraged me to read. She had tried encouraging my sisters to read, but it had never worked. She bought me a set of *Anne of Green Gables*. I loved those chronicles. Just the smell of the paper was beautiful. I was hooked.

Becoming a teenager had its challenges. The girls in my family did what most girls did; they shaved and waxed their legs, underarms, and bikini line. They shaped their eyebrows and tinted their eyelashes. They had manicures and pedicures. This was all too much for me. When menstruation started, I called my brother into the family bathroom. "I have to show you something."

Intrigued, he came in. He watched me open the bottom drawer of the cabinets.

"Ooh," he said. This drawer was off-limits; it was the girl's drawer, and he knew it. Now, I was becoming an older girl. I had graduated. I took out a tampon.

"Watch this."

I turned on the tap, putting the tampon under the running water. It blew up like a balloon.

"Amazing. How does it do that?"

"Cool, huh?" was all I said.

I never told him what females had to do with it to make it do that. I thought it was all very disgusting. It wasn't so cool when I had to use one for the first time. My sister Tegan and Mum gave me a quick explanation over a cup of tea, and off to the bathroom I went. Having it explained was one thing, but using one was quite another. I was not doing that. I returned to the kitchen, where Tegan and Mum were waiting.

"Never! Not going to happen," I told them. They laughed.

"You're such a prude," they said.

―

I helped Tegan with everything; I helped her study for her L's, I helped her when she wanted to become a chef, and I learned French so she could ace her exams. I went everywhere with her, all the time. I hung out with her friends while she would go off and leave me in the car, only to come back hours later and yell for me to get in the car so that we could go. Deep down, she hated taking me with her, but she didn't want to go alone, so she took me with her. I was called 'koukla,' which means 'doll' in Macedonian. We had many Macedonian friends. Tegan hated me for it. I got a lot of attention from boys, but I wasn't interested, and being a koukla and a much younger sister meant you were off-limits anyway. It was a good thing I was off-limits because when Tegan left me in the car, she did so because she was going off to have sex with older guys. I was left in the company of older boys, but nothing ever happened to me.

Looking back on those days, I realise just how selfish and irresponsible my sister was. One night, the whole family was invited to my uncle's house for a get-together. Tegan went downstairs into the rumpus room to retrieve something she'd left there. While she was down there, my Nanu grabbed her breast. He was drunk. She told my parents when we got home, and my father said his father would never do anything like that. He refused to believe her. She didn't get any support when she needed it. She never attended a family function ever again.

Tegan's and my ideas about boys were very different. I liked her friends and helping her study, but I started noticing how selfish she was. It was all about her. When it was my turn to study for my L's or the HSC, she was "too busy."

Amanda, my older sister, was having sex at twelve years of age. A younger relative of one of my parents' friends sometimes babysat us when my parents had to go out at night. He was eighteen. Tegan was eleven when she walked in on Amanda and the babysitter having sex, doggy style. When Amanda decided to move out with him some years later, there was a huge family fight. I suspect my parents knew of her early introduction to sex, but if they had ever tried to do something about it, I never knew. Looking back on this now, I am appalled; this was a crime because Amanda was a minor.

I was pleased Amanda was moving out because it meant that I got to have her room. I helped move her stuff. It was while my sisters and I were going through Amanda's stuff in the drawers that I found a half cucumber with a tissue wrapped around one end. I didn't understand, and I held it up to show Tegan. Tegan started screaming with laughter and told me to drop it straight away.

"But why? Why does she have this in her drawer?" Tegan explained. I was repulsed.

"At least you're holding the end with the tissue and not the other end!" Tegan screamed.

I couldn't believe I'd just touched something that had been used in such a way. I was fifteen and not *au fait* with such things. I dropped the cucumber in disgust.

My mother, who had heard the screeching and laughter, entered the room.

She asked us why we were making so much noise. "Look what we found," Tegan said.

My mother looked. She paused, looking shocked, before she said, "Put that in the bin, and we will never speak of this again."

Stunned as I was, that incident explained why my mother always wondered why we went through so many cucumbers. We were always buying extra when we went to the shops. It was an introduction to the secret world of my sister. Tegan kept a diary, but she wrote using a series of stickers. They were codes that only she understood. She let me into her world of codes so that I could read her diary and understand. Nobody else could. However, Amanda was on a different level when it came to her private life.

Amanda's 'relationship' with the babysitter continued until she was seventeen. It was an on-again-off-again affair. My father confronted the young man about the ongoing relationship and told him that he was lower than a snake for hurting Amanda whenever he broke their relationship off.

"Marry her or piss off," he said.

She ended up marrying him. It didn't last. He was violent and would break stuff when in a temper. I hated going over to their house. When his temper flared with Amanda, he'd say, "Why can't you be like Melissa?" He eventually left Amanda for her best friend. That ended the friendship as well. Nothing was ever said or done about the fact that he'd committed a crime against a minor.

Things then shifted again. Tegan was soon out in the real world, working, going to nightclubs, and hanging out with cousins her age. Everyone wanted to go to a club one night, so she gave me her ID.

"Wait out here, wait about twenty minutes, and then come in with Tony. Use my ID."

Inside she went. I went in twenty minutes later. It worked and continued to work. If I thought that our illicit behaviour would form a bond between us, I was wrong.

"Can you help me study?" I asked her. "Can you help me get my licence?"

"I'm too busy and don't want to anyway," or "I already have my licence." After a while, I stopped asking.

Not long after this, I ended up in hospital with a knee reconstruction after a very irresponsible incident with Tegan and her friends in her car. She took off when I was sitting on the boot.

I had a broken nose, a fractured jaw, gravel rash everywhere, and a black eye, which was starting to swell. Tegan kept hitting me to stay awake; we picked up Mum and went to the hospital.

When I saw the doctor, he asked me what had really happened. He thought I was a domestic violence victim. I noticed the way he had looked at Mum and Tegan's hands. They wore rings on every finger. It had occurred to him that perhaps those rings had connected with my face, but as a professional, he had seen that type of injury before and was making sure.

My jaw was wired; my nose was re-aligned. My Dad didn't see my face for two days, so by the time he saw it, the bruises were coming along. I had to continue with the story about falling down the stairs. I was black, blue, purple, stapled and stitched. Mum covered every mirror in the house so I couldn't see my face. I'd just come out of a hospital, and then Mum advised me that I was booked in to have my right knee reconstruction as soon as my face healed.

The falling down the stairs story was now becoming more of an issue. Yes, I had been advised I needed a knee reconstruction, but I kept putting it off. I remember Mum saying, "Now, I know you didn't fall down any stairs, but you need your knee fixed anyway, so it's going to happen now."

The only upside of the timing of these hospital visits was that they happened during the school holidays. Year 11 was about to start, and the following year, 1992, meant the HSC loomed up ahead. Added to that, I had just been accepted into the Australian Institute of Sport as a gymnast. My parents weren't supportive of this accomplishment, so I had to decline the offer.

I went to hospital to have my knee operation with faded yellow bruises. My jaw had healed, and my face was almost back to normal. I remember saying to Mum that I would never complain about a pimple again. The knee reconstruction saw me in hospital for six weeks. My knee problem resulted from the kneecaps sliding out of the patella. The bones wouldn't sit correctly in place.

After the operation, I was taken into my room, and my leg was strapped into a machine. The purpose of the device was to keep the leg moving. I had to lie on my back but could never lie completely flat as it hurt my back too much. The machine never stopped, even when I was sleeping. The staff would turn down the speed of the machine at night, but it still meant that sleeping was difficult. After I was discharged, I had to start rehab for my leg. In the beginning, it was excruciating. I had to do exercises to strengthen the leg and sometimes have a TENS machine on it. I was on crutches for quite some time until my leg healed. Sitting my HSC was a huge accomplishment in my eyes. Amanda had started year eleven but dropped out. Tegan and Andrew left after year ten, as they wanted to do apprenticeships. I didn't know what I wanted to do or be, so three days before I was meant to leave school in year ten, I changed my mind. I decided to go on to years eleven and twelve. I was the first and only one in my family to complete school with an HSC. Years eleven and twelve were not difficult for me, and I didn't study that hard. I did 3 Unit Art, Personal Development, Legal Studies, English, Biology, Economics, and Computer Studies. Finding out I didn't have to take Maths was a massive weight off my shoulders, one I looked forward to telling my Dad when asked. "What maths are you doing?"

With a heavy heart and a massive sigh, I replied, "No maths. I, unfortunately, wasn't able to fit maths in my curriculum."

I thought using big words like 'curriculum' would stump him, and it did, and he never asked me anything about Year eleven or twelve again. My parents would just look at me and shake their heads in disbelief when anything about the HSC arose. I thought they might have said something positive to show how proud of me they felt, but no.

"Out of all our kids, we just can't believe it's Melissa doing the HSC," my mother would say. "She's usually hopeless!"

No one helped me with study.

"I'm too busy to help you; I have a life," Tegan told me. "Whatever, get a job," Andrew said.

Only Amanda was positive. "I'm so proud of you," she said.

5. Going Places

I was still working at Target when I met James. James worked for a company that managed a shopping centre. It was 1993. I had completed the HSC by this time. While on my way to work, I saw a young man bend over to pick up some rubbish in front of me. I remember thinking that he had a cute bum, and I had the idea that I would marry him someday. I found out he had a girlfriend. That didn't bother me; it was just a matter of time, and I had lots of it. It wasn't going to take me long to move her along and be in the picture. I wasn't so shallow as to be attracted to him because of a cute backside. I'd heard the other girls in the office talking about him, and although I didn't know at the time that it was the same guy I'd seen, the talk was positive. I certainly was persistent.

My parents were quite negative about my new love focus. I wanted them to show interest, and to ask questions like other families did. Their thoughts were that it was only a matter of time before I would lose him and that I was too much of a 'fruit loop' to be able to be in a relationship.

"It won't last," my mother said. "She'll stuff it up," she told everyone. "She's a fruit loop," she said.

Looking back, I can now laugh at some of the things I did. Today, what I did would be called 'stalking.' My self-esteem was very low, and imagining I could attract a guy like James became my mission. If he could see positive attributes in me, then wasn't I worth something? I was determined to have him.

I worked out early that James was not as strong as I was. Therefore, I was prepared to take the blame for his breaking up with his girlfriend at the time. I knew he wouldn't have had the strength to accept any responsibility, so I didn't mind taking the blame. I should have seen this weakness as a warning sign, but I was smitten with him and put him on a pedestal. I was in love with the idea of being in love with him.

He would often come to see the Store Manager. I always knew when he was coming as the internal switchboard would light up with every department ringing me to tell me he was coming. I would check the cameras to see where he was and watch him make his way to the office. And still, I had the nagging thought that nobody would ever be interested in me.

"I'm not useless. I'm not. I'm not. I've got some good qualities, haven't I?"

"Yes, Melissa, you have. But what makes you think he'd be interested in you?"

I had decided sometime before that I was not going to university. I longed to start living in the real world, and so had an interview with David Jones and was accepted as one of only a few in their traineeship management program. I wasn't one who enjoyed having my head in textbooks. I knew I had excellent organisational skills, and I had determination as well. In many ways, I was quite mature for my age.

Leaving Target was not something I was thinking of doing. I thought that I could work at David Jones during the week and at Target on the weekends, but my bosses at Target believed it was a conflict of interest as DJ's were their competition. (Still don't understand that one!) I resigned from Target and was sad to leave. It would now be more difficult to see James. I started at David Jones in 1994. Part of the traineeship was a three-month indoor training period before I was given the green light to start working in our allocated stores. I was assigned to the Market Street store, and my first position was on the Ground Floor in Men's underwear. I thought they were joking. They weren't. At least the training class got a good laugh.

I loved the Market Street Store. I had many happy memories of going into the store with my Nanny. She would always wear what she called her Sunday Best and visit David Jones. The store had so much history behind it. Working in men's underwear was a real eye-opener for someone who had lived a very sheltered life. Training to be a manager meant you had to be prepared for anything and everything.

Some men asked me to measure the inside of their legs as if they were being measured for a suit. Men asked if they could go into the changing rooms together to try on underwear. It was a very steep learning curve.

I moved up in the company very quickly. I was given the opportunity to do the Market Street Easter Outposts on the ground and first floor. An outpost is a space where the top-performing gifts are placed in one area with lots of chocolate. I spent time in the Elizabeth Street store as well. I would bring many items across, products that I believed would sell. Whatever I liked, I got. I hijacked a men's underwear storage room for my outpost storage. I would smell like a giant chocolate walking around. I was given this job for several years, and I loved walking through the Elizabeth Street store and taking what I wanted. Learning about profits and loss and marketing was fascinating. I felt that marketing might be the career for me.

I progressed to other departments, spending time in Kitchenware and learning more about ordering and computer skills. I spent time in gift-wrapping, an enjoyable place to work, as long as it wasn't Christmas time. My next posting was China and Glass. The China and Glass department was mostly leased out. The light there was always dimmed. Spotlights or downlights were used to give the pieces a more attractive look and perhaps to justify some of the crazy price tags. I honestly don't know how there weren't a lot of breakages. I again took on more responsibility, working with all the staff. I would print out the sales figures from the previous day and discuss them with the department. Most of the staff wore black, but a few had corporate uniforms they had to wear.

I got to spend some time in the Gift Registry and assist brides-to-be in setting up their registries. My next department was Electrical, where I learned about plasma, DVD players, computers, movie cameras, and more. I worked on the floor a lot more, interacting with customers. It is true when buying bulky goods, be it a male or female, customers always prefer a male salesperson. I could sell a bulky or technical product just as well as any man, but sexism prevailed towards females selling this equipment. This was the first floor that paid commissions, which were certainly appreciated. I always loved it when someone knew what they wanted and needed someone to ring it up. They were my favourite sales. I learned as much as I was going to in my position, and when my traineeship was finished, I was offered an Assistant Management position, which meant using all the skills I had learned in the past eighteen months.

I progressed in my career because of my hard work ethic. At the time, I thought Mum was proud of me, but much later, I realised that it was all about status and her being able to tell all her friends about her daughter rising through the ranks.

The times that made me love my job were those where I could make a customer happy by going out of my way to do something for them beyond the usual. It made my day.

I stayed with David Jones for nineteen months before landing the role that started my career path in 1996. While working for David Jones, I would catch the train home. Mum was always waiting to find out if I saw James. She knew I was crazy about him, but she also reminded me to be careful as some of my actions could be labelled stalking. I had heard on the grapevine that he had broken up with his girlfriend. My informant was someone at the shopping centre. Finding out about the breakup confirmed it was time to make a move.

Mum, Amanda and I were shopping one afternoon and were just about to leave the centre when we ran into him. Without discussing it with me, Mum invited him around for dinner that night. I couldn't believe it. Amanda and Mum urged me to ask James to drive me home. I was not doing that, so Mum said, "If you don't, you can find your own way home because I'm not driving you." Dinner that night turned into something much bigger than I had expected.

Suddenly, everyone who had plans to go out that night now cancelled them. Nan and Grandad were invited to dinner. Amanda, who now lived out of home, was coming over, and Andrew changed his plans to stay home. Everyone was interested in meeting this James guy. Poor James fielded questions from everyone while I sat there thinking that maybe this was the last time I would see him. He handled my family with diplomacy, answering every question and asking questions of them as well. He felt comfortable around my family. The only person who didn't speak much was me. My Dad, who was usually not very talkative, talked to James all night. My mother fluttered about, chatting all night as though she was the one with a prospective boyfriend. Unusually, she seemed nervous.

As soon as James had left that night, Dad started referring to him as 'the suit.' My brother and sister said they could not understand what James was doing with me.

"Melissa is a nut case. She might be eye candy, but she will screw this up, and he's really cute."

Mum could not stop smiling. Everyone approved of James, but they were waiting for me to make a mess of the situation.

After that night, James and I started spending time together. "Let's just see her screw this one up," my mother said.

In 1996, thanks to James, I secured an interview with the national marketing manager of the company he worked with. I had made many calls but had received the usual, "We will keep your resume on file, and if anything comes up, I'll let you know." James had given me inside information about where the manager was going to be on a particular day, and I made contact with her and yet again tried to secure an interview. She sounded quite frustrated and was obviously tired of me calling, but she said she'd give me five minutes the next day to convince her that I was the person she needed in her workplace.

Our meeting went on for at least half an hour. After she'd made a quick phone call, I was on my way to a centre to meet the Centre Manager and Marketing Manager. When I arrived at the office, the Marketing Manager was sitting with his feet up at a round table. The first words out of his mouth were, "So, do you want my job?" I was shocked and quickly realised he was quite arrogant. The Centre Manager walked in and broke the ice, and finally, I could relax. The meeting went on for about half an hour. As I was leaving, I thanked them both but never thought I would see either one again. I walked out of the management office, feeling very disappointed.

I found Mum, told her about the interview, and told her the Marketing Manager was a real piece of work. I didn't want to work with him, but on the positive side, I put it down to more interview experience. I was back to David Jones the next day. Within two days, I received a call to say the job was mine if I wanted it. I resigned within a minute of getting off the phone. Mum was meeting me for lunch that day. When she got to the store, we were very busy. She asked if I had heard anything. Too busy to talk, I showed her my resignation letter and finished serving before heading off to lunch with a massive smile.

I started working in a shopping centre in Sydney as the Casual Leasing Co-ordinator/Marketing Assistant. I enjoyed my job and learned a lot from my Marketing Manager, even though I was afraid of him. There were three people on our team. The Marketing Manager, the Assistant Marketing Manager, and me, the Casual Leasing Coordinator /Marketing Assistant.

I learned a lot from both managers, but I spent most of my time learning from the Assistant Marketing Manager and only did things for the big boss, like making his tea. The only time he spoke to me was when he was telling me off. The person who trained me didn't do a very good job, and my option was to sink or swim. I swam. I realised that to learn anything, I had to do it myself and was determined to succeed. I found the work both interesting and challenging. I felt

I had found something for which I was totally suited. My father had instilled a work ethic in me. I took my job seriously and gave it everything I had.

I soon realised I was very good at my job. I was making the owners money, which had not been done before. My manager, however, continually told me I wasn't doing an excellent job and that the girl before me had done a better one. They were good friends, and she was finally promoted to another centre. She lasted about five months. One day, I walked into my boss's office to show him how much money I had made that month. I was so proud of myself. I couldn't believe it when he said, "You didn't do that; Diane did. Maybe you should stop trying to get credit for someone else's work."

I could barely believe what I was hearing. I left the room to print out Diane's work, her past year, the year and monthly projections, and my year as it stood. I placed both documents on his table and said only four words as I walked out. 'Her work. My work,' I said. I left the room, and from that minute on, our relationship changed for the better. I didn't have to prove that I could do the job; I was doing the job, and now that I had stood up to him, he finally saw I was not only doing the job but doing it better than it had ever been done before. It had taken a lot of emotional energy to stand up to him, but things changed for the better once I did.

To further my career, I started studying marketing at night. During this time, I was always sick, always on the toilet or vomiting or both. I was soon diagnosed with a phenomenon called 'dumping.' This syndrome occurs when food, especially sugar, moves too quickly from your stomach into your small bowel. I would skip breakfast and eat at noon because the girls in the office would make me. Within ten minutes, it was all out of my system. Then, there was a lot of pain. I was feeling sick and sore. Dinner was then not an option. I'd try to eat breakfast the following day, but it would not stay in my body either. It was like a merry-go-round.

James started visiting my parents' home a lot and began waiting for me after work so that he could take me home. We started dating casually. It was very low-key. I was so infatuated with him that I didn't notice that things from the beginning were unusual. I was very much a focused and determined person with my ideas, beliefs, one-year goals and my life plan mapped out. I had these plans even before I met him. I was used to an unusual and dysfunctional mother, and perhaps my goals and determination were my protection mechanisms.

On our first date, my sisters kept a watchful eye, so panic took over even before he had made his way to the front door. My mother met him at the front door. She was very chatty with James. James had packed huge coats and planned to take the ferry to Manly and back. Unfortunately, he hadn't checked the ferries' schedules, so we didn't go. I was glad about this as my hair would have been a mess. We ended up at the Opera Bar. I was extremely nervous. Over a pot of tea for two, which I almost split all over myself, we had a polite conversation and many laughs later, and we realised we had a lot in common. He said it was getting late, so he'd better get me home. I was home by 9.30 pm.

On the second date, he suddenly said, "Do you want to see my house?" I thought he was talking about one of the many he admired in the Vaucluse area. Soon, we were travelling in the opposite direction. It was dark, and we had turned off the main road and were now travelling down an almost dirt road with bushland being the only thing I could see. I was getting scared. I wanted to marry this guy, but then all thoughts of marriage disappeared. Maybe I had misjudged him. Perhaps he was a violent pervert. I didn't want to marry him at that moment. I just wanted to live. He stopped the car in front of a house and said, "There it is. My house." He had meant his real house all along. I started to breathe again. We didn't go inside and instead drove back to my parents' house. I was home by 9.30 pm once again. Even my father started asking if James really liked me. On the third date, he arranged to come past after work and wanted to sit down and discuss his goals. After going through the many pages that he had written about his life plan, he asked me if the goals he had interested me and if I could work with them. It was all very mapped out and structured.

I was inspired and wanted to know more. I liked him and thought he knew what he wanted. He was almost five years older than me. I went along with the goals and even spent time writing mine. I felt inspired. It was my first real relationship. I had no idea.

Things went well, and we had a lot of fun. I learned a lot and continued to learn things I still use to this day. I found writing out goals was meaningful, and it gave me the impetus to accept challenges. I learned about myself and my strengths and weaknesses. Writing down my goals kept me accountable.

I was soon promoted in my field and kept climbing the company ladder. I was very focused on the company's goals, and I was determined to deliver them. I had found something I was very good at, and so I put all my effort into the job.

"She's doing well because of him," my mother said.

I was doing well because I'd found something that I was very skilled at, working hard to learn as much as possible and studying at night to further my skills. I didn't bother to challenge my parents' mantras about why I was doing well. I was so used to being put down that it was normal for me to hear such comments. In my first year with the company, I earned nineteen thousand a year. I did so well for them that they raised my salary to twenty-eight thousand that first year.

One night, I was at James' parents' house when his Dad asked if I would stay for dinner. They had just ordered pizza. I said thanks but told them I'd better be getting home. Eating in front of James for the first time was too much to contemplate. James walked me to the door and followed me to the car. He got in, and we talked for about half an hour; then, suddenly, he reached over and kissed me. Before I could say anything, he was out of the car and almost opening his front door. I couldn't believe what had just happened. I was taken aback but excited at the same time. I had to pull myself together, get home as fast as possible, and tell Mum. She approved of him. I smiled all the way home. I think the car was on automatic pilot as I can't remember the journey home.

"He's a bit out of your league," my mother said when I told her. "He isn't," I replied.

She made a noise in the back of her throat. I left the room.

Although Mum seemed pleased with the new man in my life, it didn't stop her from criticising me in front of James. The first time she made negative comments about me, I thought James might suddenly spring to my defence, but he didn't. The first time my mother called me a 'bitch' in front of him, he didn't seem shocked or surprised. We had both been brought up to be respectful to older people, but I was hurt that he had no response. When I asked him why he was silent, he said he didn't want to be rude to my mother. I thought he might say something when we were alone in the car, but he didn't.

"Everybody loves Melissa," my mother would say. "It's all about Melissa."

I couldn't understand why James couldn't hear the sarcasm in her voice. Perhaps he did but chose to ignore it. Perhaps this weakness came from the fact that James and his father rarely stood up for themselves in front of James's grandmother, who could be a difficult old lady. There was only one time when they told her off because she had not seen me come in and say hello to her. They knew that I had said hello, and they set her straight. I was so smitten with him that I didn't see that there were two of us who couldn't stand up to my mother.

Despite this, our relationship deepened. We did the usual things, such as weekends together and weekend holidays. Boyfriends were never allowed on family holidays, but James was always invited. It was a given that James was coming. He always came on our yearly family holiday, but we had separate rooms. Males slept in one room, and females slept in another. My father now finally had a mate who loved fishing as much as he did and a guy who loved his daughter, even though he and no one else in the family could understand why. James had integrity and motivation and, above all, was a good person. Dad could see that, and that made him happy. My mother was besotted with him. At times, she was almost flirtatious in her manner, but I didn't take much notice of that as I was so used to her extremes of behaviour. It was just the way she was.

I was moving up in my career around this time. In addition to the Marketing Manager position, I also did some other positions that had been left when other staff left the company. For a while, I was working in the role of Marketing Manager, Assistant Marketing Manager and Casual Leasing Coordinator/Marketing Assistant. I made so much money for the company that they created a national role for me. This meant that I was in charge of all of the centres in Australia. It was a challenging role. I worked from six in the morning until late at night. Eventually, the company hired other people for all of the other roles. Two centres that had previously struggled to meet their targets were now making money. I now had people who worked under me, and I was making some quite important decisions.

As part of my new seniority, I sometimes had to get tough when staff weren't doing the job properly or when problems arose. I always gave warning letters first and tried to make my staff understand where they had gone wrong. I always tried to think outside the square when a problem came up. The last resort was to fire someone, but sometimes, there was no other option.

Firing someone was not difficult for me. I knew that every job had its good and bad aspects, and no one wanted to fire people, but the people I fired were often lazy and incompetent and doing personal things during work time when they should have been working for the company. Some of these people went on to find other jobs where they were paid more (I don't know how!) At that time, plenty of jobs were around, and they were easy to walk into. There wasn't the stress about interest rates, housing and rental shortages, and job security that there is now. It never crossed my mind to wonder what they thought of me, and I didn't feel sorry for having to sack the lazy ones when I was working so hard.

In retrospect, I sometimes wonder if I was disengaged from other people's feelings because I was hardened from an early age. I had to be tough to survive in the household I was raised in and so was tough in the business world. I'm not that tough person anymore. Later on, I had to make changes to the way I survived and leave that hardness behind.

I climbed the corporate ladder for the next few years. I enjoyed dressing up for work in suits and heels, and my self-esteem grew as I became more successful. I wasn't a useless girl who would never achieve anything. I was proving them all wrong. Doing the job I was doing didn't leave me much time for those negative comments battered into my head since childhood to creep in. I was a woman with power in my working hours. By this time, James had left Target and had joined the company.

"I'm doing it. I'm climbing up!" I said to myself.

"Make sure you don't fall, Melissa."

"I'm not going to fall or fail. You'll see."

My family could see that I was moving up quickly in my career. I was travelling a lot more with the job. They knew I was now making good money. I never discussed my salary with them as I didn't want to be accused of showing off or trying to make others jealous. I didn't buy flashy cars and jewellery. I was the same person I'd always been. All I ever discussed was the promotions I got and the type of work involved in my new role. Even then, I kept it subtle. Unless people were in marketing, they wouldn't understand what my job entailed. I knew my family thought that I had it all.

James and I went on holidays together after a while. We always had two double beds every time he booked or organised the holiday. It became a long-standing joke. We went together to Ayers Rock, Pacific Palms, Great Keppel, Port Stephens, and many other places. Because of my role in the company, I was given money to buy a car, went interstate quite a bit, stayed in very up-market hotels, and enjoyed the perks that came with the job. My parents never gave me credit for my rise to the top.

"It's James," they said. "She's lucky to have him. She's doing so well because of him. We can't believe it. Thank God for James."

I didn't bother arguing with them or correcting their impressions. I was used to being treated like I didn't have any of my own skills. It was just how it was. By the third year with the company, I was making a lot of money, much more than James.

Because I was the boss, there were times when I had to override decisions made by my staff and that included James. Sometimes, there were altercations between staff, and I would be called down to sort it out. I would listen to both sides and then make a decision. At times, I would have to agree with the person James disagreed with. It was purely a business decision. My job was to do what was best for the company. At home, we didn't discuss what had happened at those times when I had to go against James in favour of his colleagues. We both understood it was nothing personal. James and I had an agreement that while we were in the car, we could talk about work until we reached the tollbooth on the highway, and after that, it was banned.

James was an excellent worker, but sometimes I had to override him on decisions and he didn't like it. And underneath, he resented me earning a higher salary.

Every year, my salary increased.

The opportunity for a six-week trip to America came up. I decided to let James go, thinking that six weeks away from me would be a reasonable amount of time for him to realise how much I meant to him and perhaps know that he could not live without me. We had been dating for four years at that time. I'd heard that absence makes the heart grow fonder, and I wanted to see if time away would make him see he couldn't live without me.

Despite the length of time, we had been going out, which indicated that it was a serious relationship, my mother continued to make disparaging remarks about how I would stuff it up one day. I hadn't stuffed it up in four years, so I wondered why she thought I would eventually do that. It didn't make sense. James never stood up for me when my mother said the things she did. I asked him repeatedly why he wouldn't, but he couldn't give me a satisfactory answer. I came to believe that his reluctance was because he didn't want anyone to be unhappy with him.

"Don't worry about it," he'd say.

'If you marry James, then we'll give you all the love you've ever wanted,' my mother said.

I wanted my parents to love me as much as they loved my sisters and brother.

When James returned from six weeks in America, I wanted to hear two words: *Marry me*. Instead, it was back to work, long hours, night study, and work commitments. He was doing what he wanted on the weekends, and if I was willing to fit in with his plans, I was more than welcome to attend. I look back now and think I should have gone to America.

I was still a virgin at nineteen. I had always wanted my first time to be with someone special. James had been hurt badly by his ex-girlfriend, and he'd decided he would not let anyone walk all over him again. My feelings for him were so strong that I let him walk all over me. He was not flexible when it came to fitting me in with what he was doing. He put up barriers to protect himself. After a while, this began to irritate me, but I believed I could show him that I was different and deserved to be let in. Slowly, things changed. The walls started to come down.

Things went smoothly for a while, and then we started fighting about everything and nothing. The time had come to either make a long-term commitment or break up. My pride would not have allowed us to get back together if we had decided to take a break, so instead of breaking up, we decided to stay together. Looking back, I should have had a break to assess our feelings about long-term prospects.

I was too young and didn't know what I was doing. I didn't want to lose him. I loved James and thought I couldn't live without him. James was working, studying and doing whatever he wanted on weekends, and other men started to notice me. This made me feel good about myself.

"I'm not what Mum says. Men look at me," my inner voice said.

"Yes, they do. Think positively, Melissa. You are smart and attractive. You're going places."

"Yes, I am. I'm a good person. A good person. I'm a good person."

I felt special; it was nice not to be taken for granted. A man I met at work thought I was attractive and deserved attention. I would be lying if I said I didn't like the attention or him. I started enjoying seeing this other person at work events. From the first time we set eyes on each other and spoke, it was instantaneous. Christopher and I had an instant connection. I didn't have to put on a mask for him and felt I free. I could be totally honest with him and he with me.

I was now in a terrible mess. Christopher was the one for me, but I felt I couldn't get out of the situation I was in, and my parents were so enamoured with James that I couldn't tell them what was really going on in my heart. I also wanted to prove my mother wrong; I was going to show her I wouldn't stuff it up. I employed Christopher for events. He ran his own company. Part of the reason for employing him was I wanted to see more of him. He asked me to be with him, but I told him I couldn't. He accepted this. Nothing ever happened between us, but he was in my head a lot of the time.

It was a confusing time. I loved James, but I wasn't in love with him. I didn't understand what I was doing. Feeling hurt, I just wanted him to notice me and want me. I had always believed in the old-fashioned custom of the man asking the woman to marry him, and when that wasn't happening, I made up my mind to do things differently. In my head, I could hear my mother's voice, telling me that I would stuff things up and that it wouldn't last. I pushed them to the back of my mind.

I decided to send James a box of his favourite cupcakes. I couriered them to his work marked to his attention. He would unwrap the brown paper, and in thick black marker, he'd see the words: Marry Me. He called me and said he'd received the cupcakes but that I had incorrectly spelled his Mum's name and then laughed. His Mum's name was Mary. I told him I hadn't misspelled anything and hung up. I was in disbelief, crushed and hurt. I felt so empty. James didn't understand, and he never would. I decided to meet up with Christopher. We didn't do much more than kiss, but I felt terrible about it. I needed to feel as though someone was noticing.

The fights between James and me were starting to get worse. He knew something was wrong. He asked me if I was seeing anyone else, so I came clean and told him that I'd kissed someone. He was devastated, and we both cried.

I was angry with myself. I should never have kissed someone else and knew that was not the answer but not standing up for myself was worse.

For weeks, we went back and forth, trying to fix our problems. He took me away for the weekend and showered me with gifts. One night, I saw a bright star outside our room shining back at me. I told him it was my Nan, looking down on us. We had just lost her on 30th August, the same day as Lady Diana passed away. Nan loved the royal family, so this made it more special. There was another star which was a lot fainter than Nan. James said it was his Pa, telling my Nan to turn her light out. It was a very special moment.

The next day, we were leaving but decided to take one last walk around the golf course at the resort before we left. We got to the ninth hole when James turned and asked me to marry him. I had wanted this for so long, yet when it finally happened, I felt flat. With everything that had gone on and was still going on, I knew it wasn't right. It didn't feel right, so I said no. I didn't think he was genuine with that proposal. He was clutching at straws. James had another surprise waiting for me: horse riding. I had always wanted to do this, and he had arranged for us to do it. I appreciated that very much.

We had a massive argument at my parents' home one night, and before leaving, and because he was crying, my parents spoke with him. Very quickly, my parents were in my bedroom, telling me some home truths.

"You are lower than a snake," my father said. "James is too good for you. You don't deserve such a good man."

For once, Mum let Dad do all the talking. She stood, nodding her head in agreement with everything he said. I knew she was behind my father talking to me like that. My father never spoke like that to me. Later, she started her tirade.

"You're a whore. He deserves someone better."

The next time I saw my parents, I felt very uncomfortable, but they acted as though nothing had happened. I was still hurting about the way my father had spoken to me that night and that my mother had called me a whore. After I had left my parents' house, I went to James' place. I told him I loved him, and I wanted to be with him. Things settled down, and we both went back to our careers. We felt as though the future was going to work out for us as a couple, but underneath, I felt I would never breathe again.

James was driving me home one night, but home wasn't his destination. I had been feeling quite sick and just wanted to get home. We'd both had a very long day. It was 11 November 1997. I closed my eyes, and eventually, James stopped the car, speaking as he was getting out. "Melissa, please, can you get out and come over here?"

I opened my eyes, and instead of seeing my parent's suburban street, I saw the ocean. The sound of the waves crashing against the rocks is usually a sound I love, but right then, I wasn't feeling it. As I got out of the car, all I did was complain. James wanted me to sit down at the edge. Cliff edges and I were not a good mix. The wind was enough to blow me over. I stayed as far away from the edge as possible. I sat on a rock, and James came and sat with me. He gave me a card, and suddenly, he unbuttoned his shirt to reveal a white tee shirt underneath emblazoned with the words, 'WILL YOU MARRY ME?' I remember the moment so clearly.

All I could think about was what my parents had said just days ago. While crying, I told him, "Yes."

I wasn't crying with happiness, however. There was no turning back now. I realised in that moment James must have been discussing ideas with others. I had told Amanda many times I wanted to get a tee-shirt with the words I LOVE JAMES printed on it. James then handed me a shirt, which said YES. I was stunned. What happened to 'No' or 'Maybe'? I felt hurt that I hadn't had a voice in this event. Obviously, other people, including my family, knew about this, and although it may have been regarded as a lovely surprise, it wasn't.

In hindsight, I realised how naïve I was. I was twenty-two years old. I was not only doing what my parents wanted, but I was perhaps going to wreck James' life as well as mine. I often wonder if I'd dared to say 'no' how different our lives would have been.

I wanted to go to his parent's first, but as he was driving, he wanted to go straight to mine. Unbeknown to me, everyone already knew. His parents, brother, and all my family were there. Mum was crying, and I saw his Dad smile for the first time. Finally, I was doing something right, and at that moment, I wasn't the family fruit loop, loser or 'useless.' I was the one they looked at and smiled at. Mum had even set out the good room for a celebration dinner. Everything had been planned without any input from me. I felt as though something had been stolen from me. I had no voice in this arrangement. I felt ripped off, and all

I could think about was the other man who was right for me. Imagine what an awkward moment it would have been if I had said no.

Everyone was in a celebratory mood. The only awkward person was me. I felt as though I was being pushed in a particular direction, and I wasn't ready. Tegan was getting married in the near future, so I thought that might buy me some time. I was wrong. Not long after the celebrations, James and I were returning from visiting some of his cousins on the Central Coast when my mobile rang. It was my mother.

"I've called the church, and there are only two dates left, April the 15th and May the 9th. Which one?"

"Hi Mum, actually we were thinking of later in the year or early next year. I just need some time."

I was trying to prolong it for as long as possible.

"There's no time to wait, no need for long engagements; six months is long enough. Choose one, or I'll choose one for you. Melissa, I want an answer right now, and remember, the wedding date is the starting point for everything else."

"But Mum, there's so much happening. We just need a little more time together before that."

"A date, Melissa. Now!"

"The 9th of May, Mum," I said, and with that, she hung up. I turned to James and told him our wedding date had been chosen. He thought the date related to the following year. I told him it didn't. He nodded. We had a lot to organise. I picked the second date Mum suggested as it was the furthest away and gave me a little bit more time to think about getting out of the whole thing.

Our engagement party was held on 10 January 1998.

Around this time, I had begun to notice that, at times, my eyes seemed to be playing tricks on me. Sometimes, I couldn't tell if a car was stationary or was moving. It happened when I was driving quite a few times, but I didn't think much about it; I had a wedding to plan, and I just put it down to one of those weird things that your body does at times, and perhaps it was due to stress or knowing that I was marrying the wrong man. I pushed the problem to the back of my mind. I had a wedding to organise. There was a lot to be done. It's just tiredness and stress, I told myself. It'll all work out, even though a little voice was telling me it was the wrong decision. I chose to put it down to stress.

6. Whose Wedding?

With our wedding date already decided, Mum was back working with Tegan to finalize Tegan's big day. Tegan's wedding was five weeks before ours. Thankfully, with Mum being so busy, James and I were left to organise what was left of our wedding day.

James was very hands-on. He prepared a spreadsheet that listed all the tasks he could think of that needed to be done. He would fax it to me to add or make any changes and add deadlines. I would send him daily 'Honey to-do lists.' I had decided to have a hyphenated name. I was proud of my Maltese heritage and liked my family name.

"No way," my mother said. "James and I are against it. You'll do the traditional thing and take your husband's name."

As disappointed as I was and irritated that my mother and James had obviously had that discussion, I reluctantly agreed. Between the two of us, our wedding was coming together. We were getting married in an Anglican church. Although I was Catholic, I believed that God wouldn't care where we got married. It could be in a park, pool, picnic ground, or patio. It was the commitment that counted. When Nan passed away, there had been the usual discussion about coffins and plots. Mum suggested that the burial take place in the Anglican part of the cemetery. Grandad did some research and found that burial in the Catholic part was cheaper, so that was the deciding factor regarding her resting place.

James and I worked well together on wedding planning. With the countdown on and my sister's wedding over, my brother's birthday was the only event before our big day. Final checks were made, and tasks were being ticked off the spreadsheet. I had been at work from 6 am one morning and was finalizing the reception. I had spent a lot of the day on last-minute details when my mobile phone rang while I was driving. I stopped at the lights.

It was Christopher. We spoke for a while, and I felt I could finally breathe for the first time in a long time. I could see us together forever. It was just us in that moment; my current world washed away. He could see the real me, no masking. But negative thoughts filtered through my head and were easier to believe.

"Don't get married to him. Marry me."

I wanted to go to him. The lights had changed; I hadn't noticed but drove on autopilot. I was shocked. I wanted to be him so much. Eventually, I was pulled over by a policeman and fined for speeding. I couldn't believe I was speeding, but I just copped it on the chin and had a good cry. I couldn't entertain the idea of stopping the marriage. The wedding preparations were too far gone.

There was so much to do; I didn't have a lot of time for reflection. I had always thought that if I got married, I would have my boss as my Matron of Honour. I'd have my first cousin on Mum's side and my best friend as my bridesmaids and a page boy and a flower girl. My mother put a stop to those wishes.

"You have to have your sisters in the bridal party. Amanda would be devastated, and what about Tegan?"

I tried to reason with her, explaining that Tegan was getting married only a few weeks before me and had told me she'd be too busy with her own wedding. My mother was adamant about me asking Amanda. My bridal party ballooned into a circus of fifteen people. I didn't want that many people, but Mum overrode me. We all met at a shopping centre one morning with my aunt, cousin and sisters. It was one of the centres I managed, and I was sure we'd find the right dresses there.

"I'd be surprised if Melissa is capable of choosing a dress, and if she does, it will probably take forever," my mother told everyone before we got into our cars.

When we arrived, the first thing we did was to have coffee and snacks. I had been experiencing headaches in the past few weeks, and that morning I had one. My eyes were still playing tricks on me, but once again, I put it down to running around too much with the wedding organisation.

"After all, we'll need all our strength because she'll probably take all day to find a dress. You all know what *she's* like," my mother said.

I already had an idea of the store I wanted to buy the dresses from. We emerged from that store with everyone in agreement over dresses, ice-blue bodices and skirts. Tegan had stepped in for my best friend, who couldn't make it that day. They were the same size. Now Tegan decided she loved the dress so much that she wanted to be in the bridal party. I called James and asked him to find another groomsman. The bridal party was now seventeen people. I was losing control of my own wedding, but I reasoned that my mother would be delighted, and I wanted her to be happy and proud of me. Perhaps this was the thing that would finally get me into her good books. It was the price I had to pay to please her, to finally hope that she would appreciate and love me.

"Well, how amazing. Melissa has actually made a decision and made it in record time," my mother said.

May 9 finally arrived. There was no time to reflect on what was about to take place. My bridesmaids all arrived. My cousin, who was a bridesmaid, was now living at my parents' house. Amanda lived around the corner, and Tegan and Jess had to travel to my parents' house via car. We were off to get our hair done as soon as everyone had arrived. When we returned, it was madness. All the bridesmaids ran to their battle stations to do makeup and get dressed. My pageboy and flower girls had arrived, so dressing them and keeping them clean was going to require some supervision. My pageboy was a veteran. He'd done this before, so thankfully, he could keep the girls in check. The boys forgot their jacket flowers, so my brother had to make a mad dash and find a florist. It was Mother's Day the next day, so flowers were hard to come by.

"How does this work?" and "Where does that go?" and "Breathe in!" and "Don't breathe!" If that wasn't bad enough, I had to wear makeup.

My mother and I had spent a good hour trying to find makeup that wasn't like spackle. When we finally found one and paid for it, my mother thanked God, and I remember thinking that it was my very first make-up purchase.

"Well, well, Miss Beautiful has finally bought some make-up," my mother said.

I could hear the sarcasm in her voice, but I focused on the positive. Perhaps she would stop being so negative when she saw that I wouldn't wreck James' life by marrying him and that we could be happy together.

I had always imagined going along George Street in a stretch limousine to the church. That dream was short-lived as the driver took all the back streets. Finally, I was standing with my Dad at the church door. My stomach lurched. I suddenly didn't want to go in. It wasn't just wedding jitters either. This was something else.

As I walked down the aisle with my Dad, I realised what being loved felt like. I had never felt that before that moment. I was feeling it for the very first time. I was pulling off the one moment, which I am sure my family thought they would never see. They were all still holding their breaths until we were announced husband and wife. And yet, as I was walking down that aisle, despite feeling loved by James and finally accepted by my family, my gut was telling me that this was wrong. There was no doubt that I loved James very much, but even so, something didn't sit right within me. I knew what it was: This wasn't about my happiness and forever; it was about them, my family. It was a disturbing feeling, but I tried to overcome it and get on with the day.

Once I had signed the marriage certificate, I began to walk back to the position I was standing in before, and as I did, a ladder fell on my ankle. What was a ladder doing in St Andrew's Cathedral? They had been working on the organ, but instead of hiding it away for a wedding, someone had decided to leave it resting against a wall, thinking it was out of the way. The long train on my dress had somehow pulled the ladder over. Dad and Grandad came to my aid. Commotion reigned for a while, and soon I was on my way back to the altar in new high heels that weren't doing me any favours and now I was limping. I could feel a large bruise rising. All I could think about was – *This can't be happening.*

This was not how it was meant to be. What was I doing? I realised that this was about time and the future and biding my time till sometime in the future when I could end it. This is something you shouldn't be thinking about, especially on your wedding day. Much of that day wasn't in my control. Many elements of my wedding day had been organised by others. There were things that we were and weren't allowed to do. I loved James, but this was not 'our' wedding. I felt like I was just playing a major role in it. A wedding day is meant to be the greatest day of your life. Mine certainly wasn't. My thoughts were sometimes with another person. What have I done? I asked myself.

"Something's wrong. I don't feel like I'm supposed to feel."

"It's all right, Melissa, it's just emotion overwhelming you."

"No, it's not that. I don't feel right. What's wrong with me?"

"Calm down; it'll settle. You'll be happy."

After the service, we felt like we both just wanted to go home and rest, but there was a reception to attend. We climbed into the limousine with the page boys and girls, and quiet was out of the question. We finally arrived at the reception venue on time for a quick makeup touch-up. I was finally able to ditch the $300 high heels. We made our grand entrance to the song from *Beauty and the Beast*. The bridal party was introduced, and the first course arrived on the tables.

The toasts came. Before the wedding, I bought a book for James about speeches and what people needed to include in a wedding speech. He didn't refer to it and instead, had called my Mum and read his speech to her for reassurance. His speech was quite a few pages long, but the one thing I wanted to hear was not in it. There was nothing about how beautiful I looked. Instead, he spoke about the three 'tests' I had passed to gain his approval. The first was to see how well I mixed tuna, oil and sand into fish bait. Passed. The second was articulating my goals. Passed. The third was my fishing ability. Passed. It sounded like a talk for company reps interviewing prospective employees. He talked about how beautiful the bridesmaids looked; traditionally, that's the best man's job. The one thing that I expected him to say first, he didn't say at all. At least he thought someone looked beautiful that day.

I thought it couldn't get any worse. James' mother spoke next. I found out later that his Dad wanted to say a few words, but she hadn't allowed it. His mother's first words were, "Well, I'm losing a son." I had to sit there and smile like that didn't hurt. She wore a very dark shade of navy. It was almost black. I wish his father had spoken, as my connection with him was genuine.

Our honeymoon was hit and miss. I didn't feel connected to James a lot of the time, and I was masking having a good time. I had been to Hawaii twelve months before, so I could show him all the places to go, and we also visited new locations.

On our return to Australia, James decided to keep renting the house he was paying off to get as much of it paid as possible, so we moved into his room at his parents' house. Things started to get more difficult the longer we stayed there, as I wanted a chance to settle down and be a family in our own home. Living with my parents-in-law was all right, but I desperately wanted privacy and a place we could call our own.

I wasn't a materialistic girl. I didn't have to have the latest fashion, handbags, shoes, or jewellery. I wanted the big things, the things I think most people want:

a partner, some children, a house, a car, a career. I just wanted to live a happy and successful life. I was prepared to work hard to attain the things I thought were important.

After four months at his parents' house, we decided we needed to move.

James and I then spent six months at my parent's house.

I was twenty-three and still living at my parents with James in 1999 when I became aware that, at times, my leg or my arm would tremble. I couldn't stop it from doing this. It wasn't painful, and once again, I chose to ignore it as just another one of those weird body things, along with the problem of not knowing whether cars were moving or stationary. I put it down to overwork and stress.

If we had a fight or argument while living with my parents, James would speak to my Mum about it, and then she would berate us both. When James was wrong about something, she would tell him, but that was not very often in her eyes. Mostly, she scolded me and seemed to always agree with James. It was as though she wanted to please him, and the consequences were not good. We started fighting about living in our own house; I had had enough of living with my parents and wanted to live in our own place.

He wanted to get as much of the house paid off by the tenants. I understood this, but he was always chasing payments as the tenants were always behind in their rent, which meant he was always going to the tribunal. This situation started to irritate me the longer it went on, but he couldn't see how frustrating it was for me.

One night, we were at a family function with many relatives and friends. One of my relatives asked me how I was. Before I could answer, my mother jumped in over the top of me. I was sitting right there, and I could have answered for myself. She started by regaling all my medical stuff and then moved on to her favourite theme.

"Of all our children, can you believe it? She's doing well. Thank God for James. What would we do without him?"

James didn't say anything. There was no credit for me. I grimaced at the 'we' as if the whole family had somehow been spared a dreadful fate with the arrival of James on the scene. I didn't say anything. I was used to my mother doing this. It didn't occur to me to challenge her.

Sometime after Tegan got married, she, Mum and I were in the kitchen drinking tea. Tegan was having a few problems with her husband and telling Mum about it.

"You should be married to James, Tegan," my mother said. "He's so perfect, and Melissa certainly doesn't deserve him."

At first, I thought she was joking. Then I realised that she wasn't. It was a horrible comment to make, but I'd been listening to those comments all my life and was used to them. James wasn't perfect. Nobody was perfect; it was ridiculous. What was the point of telling my sister that she should have married my husband? To make my sister jealous of me? I filed it away with the thousands of comments that my mother had always made about me over the years and tried to forget it. I didn't understand her at all. I'd given up trying to a long time ago. James sensed my frustration with our situation and finally decided we had to move out and be on our own. He gave the tenants notice; we did an inspection and were ready to move in. There was a lot of work that needed to be done.

Cleaning the house was a big job. Mum and my eldest sister helped. Everything had to be cleaned and re-cleaned: kitchen cupboards, bathrooms, everything. My first house gifts from James were new toilet seats, as he knew I wouldn't sit on the ones the tenants had used. I took a week off work and focused on making the nightmare of a house into something beautiful that I could call our home. Finally, twenty thousand dollars later, it was time to move in.

After months of sitting on Ikea chairs, we bought a lounge and a coffee table. If my brother and his mates came over, beanbags and our blanket box were the additional seating arrangements. James didn't think we needed a lounge but agreed to look for one. I had already found a lounge and paid to have it delivered. I wanted him to like it despite him thinking we didn't need one. His attitude changed when the lounge arrived, and he could lie down, stretch out and watch TV.

I always wanted to start fixing the house as soon as we got home from Bunnings, and James just wanted to rest.

Bunnings become one of our favourite stores. I capitalized on my husband's good moods when we were at Bunnings and spent quite a lot of money. He was always surprised when we got to the register and saw the total. He was surprised that drawer handles could be so expensive, forgetting that we had also bought a new front door, which we had to pick up around the back of the store.

I wasn't the greatest of cooks, but I tried. I hadn't learned to cook from my mother because I never liked her cooking anyway.

At that time, I was on a special diet, which I hoped would fix up some of the stomach and bowel problems I was having. James complained after the first meal of the diet, declaring that he was not going to eat cardboard, so I cooked two meals at night, mine and a different one for him. By the time 1999 was drawing to an end, I was starting to experience bad headaches, along with trembling limbs and eye problems. I felt my headaches were getting worse. I was twenty-four and beginning a new life, so I didn't take my symptoms seriously at first.

Doctors had told us that we would have to wait two years to start a family if I needed a bowel operation, which was on the cards. I accepted this and looked forward to the day we could start planning for children. Sometimes, it was hard, especially when other people had good news. James' brother and his wife came over one night and told us they had been trying for a baby, and although it wasn't confirmed, they believed she was pregnant. I felt like I was dying inside. I wanted to scream and bury myself in a hole, but I had to put on a brave face and be happy for them, which I was. Nine months later, when their baby was born, I held their baby and congratulated them on their small miracle, hoping that in the future, they might be congratulating me.

Now that we were in our own home, we could relax and have some fun. We loved the beach and four-wheel driving; even when we got bogged down in mud, we didn't care. We were having fun.

Our dog would accompany us on these adventures. He'd swim in the ocean and chase his ball. Afterwards, he'd walk along the esplanade with us. Sometimes, we'd go mountain bike riding. I loved to go after it had been raining as there were more puddles to splash through and more mud. We'd go ski-kayaking on some weekends. James bought me a custom-made ski-kayak in my favourite colours. It was a lot of fun.

One of the games I'd play was in the supermarket aisle that held hygiene and toiletries. To counter the mundane activity of food shopping, I'd be very silly. James was quite discreet about things to do with the body, whereas I'd been poked and prodded so much by medical staff that I was quite blasé. When he'd tell me in a lowered voice that we needed condoms, I'd ask which type he wanted. Strawberry-flavoured? Ribbed for extra pleasure? James would look embarrassed, and I would laugh. If I saw other people nearby, I'd have a favourite saying.

"Pick the ones you want, but we'd better keep them at my place in case your wife finds out."

Some people would look disgusted, and James would go red while I laughed.

He'd pretend to look at other products while I talked loudly, which made him squirm.

Like any marriage, we had our ups and downs in those early days.

That year, I decided, with the help of his brother, to buy him a new surfboard. When James got home and saw the new board, he asked where the old one was. I told him I'd traded it for a new one. He moped for days. Seriously? I tried to repurchase the old one, but it had been sold. James was a triathlete, and even though he loved chocolate, he kept himself in good shape.

At times, my mother and my sisters would visit. One afternoon, I was sitting on the back steps, watching my niece play in the back garden with the dog. My sisters pulled up into the garage at the back, and I had already opened the garage door. I could hear them talking. They were discussing Botox and who in the family would have it.

"No way," said Amanda. "Melissa would be the first to get Botox. She's so vain!"

"Yeah, she'll be the one."

"It's always about her."

I didn't understand those comments. The times I looked in the mirror were those when I wanted to ensure I had nothing stuck in my teeth. I didn't wear make-up, preferring a more natural look. My sisters were the ones that plastered their faces with layers of make-up and bought cosmetics. On one occasion, we were looking at photographs from the past, and there was one in which the wind had made us all look dishevelled, including me.

"Look at Miss Gorgeous," said Tegan with sarcasm.

"I wasn't wearing make-up or anything!" I said in my defence.

It wasn't my fault that I looked all right, and they didn't. There was another occasion when we were meeting up to go somewhere, and once again, I wore what I considered regular day clothes. Tegan had come from working in a hot kitchen looking very dishevelled. Amanda had come from the hairdresser and was sporting a new hairstyle that didn't suit her at all.

"I didn't know we were dressing up," she said pointedly, looking at me. "I'm not dressed up," I said.

My sisters were slightly overweight, and I was slim. They had bad skin at times, whereas my skin was always clear. Nobody in the family would have needed Botox. My mother knew that I had been on an organic diet for three years, and the thought of putting a foreign substance, let alone cow botulism, into my body would have horrified me. Sometime later, I would recall that conversation under very different circumstances.

―

Christmas was always a massive event at our house. I wanted James to feel special, and I loved seeing the huge smile on his face. When he saw that most of the presents were for him, his face would light up, and my heart would leap. I bought our first tree from one of my suppliers. I always decorated it with a theme to do with colour: blue tinsel with white baubles and red hanging baubles with green tinsel.

The presents under the tree were wrapped in the same colours. James always helped his parents put their tree up, so I put up our tree alone. I don't know why he couldn't break with that tradition now that he was married. That became our tradition: Me, myself and I putting up the tree and decorating it. What was I doing, and who had I become? I was so done.

Christmas was one of his favourite times of the year; he would buy books he wanted to read throughout the year, wrap them all up individually and place them under the tree so he had more presents to open on Christmas Day.

I changed all that. I would easily spend around five thousand dollars on presents just for him. One year, I bought him a 74cm TV. My brother was a tech-head, so he had it all ready-to-go for James when he arrived home.

I brought him a lot of presents in the time we were together from small gifts of tee-shirts and underwear to expensive equipment. I would wrap each present individually, even if they came in a pack of ten. Each year, I had to make sure that my gifts would be bigger and better than the year before. I just wanted to make him happy.

I was always the more spontaneous one in the relationship. I didn't mind a dare or a risk. I invited my husband to get it happening on the dining room table one evening. It was a spur-of-the-moment decision, and he complied willingly, but the next morning, he looked at me strangely as if I had done something wrong. It happened again one afternoon when we were fishing, and we found an alcove.

"Perfect place to get it on," I said. "Come on."

"Don't be silly. Get back in the boat," he said.

I could tell he was not impressed with my suggestion by the sound of his voice, and he was silent all the way home. I thought he might have been pleased to have an adventurous partner.

I was pretty much always disappointed that all my efforts were not reciprocated, and he didn't make an effort with presents for me, getting others to buy them – things I didn't like.

James and I were both fans of several life coaches and those who shared their wisdom about building a business, networking and pursuing goals in life. We had decided that we would go together when and if Anthony Robbins came to Australia. I had the advertising brochure for his appearances in Sydney. I was out one night with my mother, sisters, and a relative. We were on our way to see the musical *Annie* at Star City Casino when I saw James and his boss walking near the Entertainment Centre. I asked them what they were doing, and James' boss told me they were going to see Anthony Robbins. It was the first I'd heard about it. James looked sheepish and wouldn't look directly at me. I felt very hurt that he hadn't told me.

"Mum and Dad bought my ticket for my birthday," he said.

It didn't lessen the hurt, and over time, I started to realise he really didn't know me at all.

7. An Inconvenient Truth

I had to travel to Canberra for a few days when an incident happened that fuelled my disappointment in James. I was in an elevator late at night in Canberra when a man inside grabbed me and pushed me up against the wall. He was drunk; the smell of alcohol filled the elevator. I tried to push him off, but his hands were all over me. He was trying to pull my skirt down, and I was trying to push him off me when the elevator doors suddenly opened. He was surprised and sprang back. He was unsteady on his feet. I ran straight to my room. My heart was beating wildly. I had to get out of the hotel. I threw my stuff in my bag, grabbed all my paperwork, and called reception to have my bill ready and my car brought up. I wasn't staying there for another minute. I called James before leaving to tell him what happened and that I was on my way home. I was shaking as I got into my car, and I knew I had to stop shaking as I had a long drive ahead of me. The only thing that kept me going was the thought that I would soon be home in a safe place.

It was almost midnight when I reached our house. The stars were still out. The house was in darkness. I wondered why none of the lights were on as James knew that I would be arriving. When I entered the house, it was in darkness. I had expected James to come out as soon as my car pulled into the driveway. He must have been up all night worrying about me. I went into our bedroom, where I found him asleep. I got in beside him and cried myself to sleep. The next morning, I woke to the sounds of James getting ready to go to work.

"Are you coming to work or staying home today?" he asked. "I can't get what happened last night out of my mind," I said.

"Owners meeting today," James replied. Gotta go, or I'll be late. It's already five a.m."

He walked out the door, and I heard the car start and the electronic gates closing.

On autopilot, I showered, dressed and drove to work. I didn't want to stay in the house alone. I can't remember the drive to work, but somehow, I got there. I tried to focus on my job that morning, but I couldn't. I'd type something and then break down crying. My workmates knew something was wrong. Never before had I shut my office door. That day, the door was shut. The office secretary was also a friend. She asked me what was wrong. I ended up telling her everything, including the fact that James obviously wanted to carry on as though nothing had happened. I'd always said that his career came first, but I didn't mean it so literally that it overshadowed a sexual assault to the point where James thought that I could just go to work as though the incident didn't matter or wouldn't affect me.

A short time later, the centre owners arrived, and I was summoned downstairs to meet with them and my boss. I expected they wanted the latest financial updates, so I had the data ready. I greeted the owners and told them that the latest figures looked promising.

"Melissa, what are you doing here? We just heard what happened to you last night. Please, go home. Take time off."

"I'm better off here. I can keep busy. I can't be in the house alone."

"Then James must also take the day off to stay with you."

"But James wrote the report that will be presented at the meeting today."

The owners and my boss shook their heads.

"Has James forgotten that he's your husband? Someone else can present the report. He's taking the day off, and that's an order."

The owners and my boss went to find James and told him he was to take time off and look after his wife. Melissa should be your only concern today, they told him.

Once in the car, James turned to me.

"You made me look weak in front of the owners," he said.

"And you made it look like I don't matter to you. And you made it look like *a sexual assault* on your wife is *not* important." 'You are inconveniencing me,' he replied.

I felt like someone had just kicked me in the guts. He hadn't even asked if I was all right or whether I needed to go to a doctor. We sat in silence for the rest of the drive home. I looked out the window while tears were streaming down my face. The words were banging in my head. Made me look weak. What about me? Surely an assault on your wife, a person you are supposed to love, is more important than delivering a report at work?

A small voice in my head told me the reason for this behaviour, but it was tough to admit that this was the reason. It was the elephant in the room, and we had never discussed it. It was this: I was in a higher role at work than James was. I was accountable directly to the owners while James was in another department with a different job description. I earned a lot more than he did. He was jealous. It was a pathetic excuse for not being concerned about a sexual assault, but I knew that it was part of the reason.

The whole episode had exhausted me. I simply shut down. I could only look after myself. I was still experiencing the strange phenomenon of not knowing whether vehicles were moving or stationary. I had weird tremors in my legs and arms at times, which I once again attributed to stress. Inside, I was seething with anger. I threw out the Canberra clothes and threw myself into work, earning even more money.

This incident was a bone of contention between James and me, the elephant in the room, but it was never discussed. It was just always hanging there.

—

I worked on the introduction of Optus in Australia and met television personality Larry Emdur, who was the MC for the occasion. It was a real highlight for me, but it was a huge day and a massive event. The company was pleased with how the event turned out. The Marketing Manager and Advertising Manager were both promoted, so the marketing team of three became a marketing team of one: me! With all the work I had to do, I was on the job from 6 am to between 6 pm and 8 pm. I had been thrown into the deep end. I had to learn both the Advertising and the Marketing Managers' roles.

I also worked on bringing one of the Central Coast's major shopping centres into the black.

I decided to have a break as I had been working far too hard and was very tired. My original centre wanted me to consult with them, so I agreed to do it two days a week as I wanted time at home. The money I was commanding was like working for two weeks instead of two days. Soon, the manager of another of my previous centres contacted me and asked me to consult for them, so I agreed.

I didn't want to reject any work offered, and I respected the centre manager and looked forward to working with her again. She had been my first manager.

My 'break' turned out to be one day plus the weekend. I enjoyed my day walking the dog, reading, shopping, catching up with my Mum and cleaning the house, which I loved doing. I love a clean house where everything has a place.

I was still always sick or depressed as I could not get any answers to my medical problems. I had been off anti-depressants for a while. James did not understand depression at all.

"You don't need anti-depressants," he said. "Come off them." I went cold turkey, which was a mistake. I felt terrible.

"You get sick, and then you get over it or get it fixed. Or you die. You don't just get sicker and sicker," he declared.

Those words stuck inside my brain. How could anyone not understand? Hasn't he ever experienced anyone getting sicker and sicker? What planet was he on? I was disappointed in his attitude. Another area that made me dispirited was the area of housework. We both had full-time jobs. James would complain if I asked him to do anything, especially on the weekend.

"I work hard all week," he said. "I want the weekends for me."

He didn't stop to think that I worked all week as well. I did all the cleaning, and I wasn't feeling well at all. Mum wouldn't help me, but she always cleaned my sister's café business. She supported the rest of her children in whatever way she could. She gave them money, helped them clean, bought them household items and ran errands. I didn't say anything, but I felt hurt that I was getting no support at a time when I needed it. I didn't think it was right that I had to drag a vacuum around while my husband sat on the lounge. It wasn't fair. My migraines were increasing, and I didn't have the energy for housework. Being raised the Maltese way meant we didn't pay for cleaning, but eventually, I hired someone to do the ironing. Nobody seemed to understand depression. Luckily for them, they had never experienced that bottomless pit of no hope.

My mother-in-law arranged a meeting with an 'environmental doctor'. Environmental medicine is a branch of medicine that examines how the environment interacts with and impacts on our bodies. Environmental medicine overlaps with other branches of medicine, including toxicology, industrial medicine, and public health.

Even though she was controlling and mean, I put my mother's behaviour down to it being 'just the way she is.' She was a contradiction, sometimes cruel, sometimes supportive. I will always cherish those treatments and the time we shared. I have fond memories of trying to fit into the toilet together at the environmental doctor's office, me sitting on the toilet seat, and Mum holding up the intravenous bag. We sure knew how to laugh about the worst things. It was just the two of us. It wasn't ever easy, but somehow, she understood.

My treatments finished, and by then, I was working with a girlfriend on a marketing re-launch / re-positioning campaign. Things were getting very hectic. I was working at Centre A on Monday mornings, Wednesday and Friday afternoons and at Centre B on Monday afternoons, and Tuesdays and Friday mornings. There was no time to think about how tired I was. My diet consisted of grazing on particular food groups I made up in small batches to take to work.

I arranged to go to Queensland to see an environmental doctor who would put me on a special diet as I was still having stomach problems. My mother and James came with me. As soon as we were in the consulting room, my mother took over, not letting me speak for myself. She took over as if she knew more than me. The doctor, who picked up on the dynamics straight away, kicked her out. She waited outside and was not impressed. She declared she didn't believe in environmental medicine and that it wouldn't do a thing.

"I don't like him," she declared later.

After the session, I went back to the hotel and took a bath. I was tired and needed to think about what the doctor had told me. My mother burst into the bathroom and accused James and me of ignoring her. I wasn't ignoring her; I was exhausted and needed a while to reflect and process all that I had heard that afternoon. I passed it off as just another one of her odd behaviours.

I wasn't allowed to have coffee but could have green and herbal tea. I felt better on the diet. I cut out sugar and was pretty strict. My energy levels went up. I believe the diet helped me, and I am convinced it helped with my eyesight problems. The environmental doctor restricted the carbs, but my personal trainer at the time was not happy. There was no way I could do the exercises the trainer had on my exercise plan because my energy levels were too low. My trainer phoned my doctor, and they had a talk. They came to an agreement about my diet, and both were happy.

When I first went on the diet, I had withdrawal symptoms. I used to sit rocking back and forth, and sometimes I'd be sweating, but after six weeks, I suddenly felt really good, and the longer I stayed on it, the better I felt. I kept the diet up for three years until I couldn't do it anymore. I was sick of taking instructions from other people. I threw my folder out with all the medical and nutritional information and resumed regular eating.

Sometimes, I would go to work on the weekends to catch up on paperwork. I would know when my system had hit overdrive when I had to travel. I'd wake up in a strange hotel room and wonder what day it was and which city I was in. It would take a few seconds to register exactly where I was and what I had to do for that day. At work on Friday mornings, I would go down to the health food store and get myself a bag of carob honeycomb. It didn't taste too good, but it was my treat for the week.

One morning, a colleague and I started our presentation, which went smoothly for a while. I was in charge of the PowerPoint presentation. My colleague had just started her own business after leaving the same company I had left, so this was her big moment. I remember touching the button on the laptop, and then everything went dark. I slid down the wall. When I opened my eyes, I saw everyone crowding around me. I had fainted. One retailer was trying to tell me I was pregnant; others were all talking amongst themselves. Someone called James to come and take me home. I had wrecked a significant night. Despite my fainting, the night was successful, and all the retailers were impressed with the campaign.

After seeing my doctor and getting the all-clear, I returned to my busy schedule. I made sure I stuck to my gluten-free diet, I continued with my shopping centre work, and things started to settle down. I was too busy to notice anything else.

One morning, when I was at one of the centres, my boss mentioned that I needed to buy suits that fitted me. I thought he was joking as I was wearing a suit I had been wearing for a while. I looked down at my pants and noticed they were gathered at the sides, and my belt was too big. I couldn't understand why. I was eating well. I was eating all day, every two hours. How could this be, and why hadn't James noticed it? Why hadn't I noticed it? Why hadn't anybody in the family said anything?

At FWH, I tried on some new pants. It was June 19, 2000. I was shocked that

I was now a size six and needed a belt to hold them up. I had work to do, and I pushed it down. I had to get to the next centre.

Occasionally, I'd have to have an injection after eating for intense pain. James and I were driving to a dentist appointment that afternoon when I experienced terrible pain. We were making good time, and I wasn't going to be late. We were almost at the dentist when the pain became unbearable. I called my specialist, who advised us to go straight to hospital. My bowel was twisted, and I needed immediate surgery. I called Mum and told her what was happening.

"I don't have time for this," she said. "I'm cooking your father's dinner, and I have your niece here."

"We're going to the hospital. The doctor said I have a twisted bowel. It's dangerous."

"Do whatever," she said and hung up.

For a split second, I couldn't believe Mum's attitude, even though she often said inappropriate things. She had always been there whenever I was sick, despite her cruel comments to me, and now suddenly she wasn't. That conversation changed it all. I realised I had to deal with it alone. I didn't mind going to hospital. I wasn't a hypochondriac, but I'd always put my hand up for an operation. Operations meant pain, and I deserved to be in pain since I was inconveniencing everyone around me. I needed to be punished. This life wasn't mine; it was theirs.

At the hospital, I was given Pethidine and hooked up to machines. Blood samples were taken. I could still feel the pain lingering, but it was finally bearable. The doctors thought perhaps it was an ectopic pregnancy. When my mother arrived, the doctor shook her hand and told her it was renal colic and I would be fine in twenty-four hours. As I was leaving the emergency department, I started vomiting all over the mat near the door. Suddenly, my pants were pulled down, and I felt the sting of a needle. I went back into the hospital, and after some time, they allowed me to go home.

I returned to my parents' house, but I could not settle. I couldn't sit still and couldn't get comfortable. Mum became angry and started shouting at me. I didn't know what was happening, but I knew the drugs were wearing off, and the bearable pain was not so tolerable anymore. I had interrupted her evening. She gave me two options.

"Go to bed and deal with it!" she shouted. "Or go back to hospital. I've got things to do."

I was distraught. It was a bitchy thing to say to a daughter who was in obvious pain. She knew that I had a high pain threshold and rarely complained, so I was shocked at her response. However, as the pain increased, I forgot all about her attitude. I took option two and returned to the hospital.

I was not admitted but spent the night in emergency where they gave me more drugs to help with the pain. I could feel a huge lump in my stomach and asked the nurse if she could see anything, but she said she couldn't. During the night, they topped up the pethidine, which helped me sleep, and I suppose it kept me quiet. They were concerned about my weight, which had dropped to thirty-seven kilos.

By morning, the lump was the size of a tennis ball, not in my stomach but in my bowel. A surgeon was quickly called to review my case and decide the next course of action. I was relieved that they started to believe my pain was real. I was quickly admitted. I don't remember everything, as they kept me sedated.

I do remember one night, James was there. He had come straight from the office and missed lunch to get as much work done as possible. I was nil by mouth but was given dinner for some reason, which James ate. I remember seeing him shovelling my dinner into his mouth when I awoke.

The pain increased. The nurses joked that they could play join the dots on my bottom due to all the injection sites. My bottom was very bony. I had bruises everywhere, and after a while, they had to start using the fronts of my legs to inject.

I never had a complete understanding of what was happening, as they kept me pretty sedated. I had a tube down my throat, which made it hard to sleep.

I heard the surgeon on the phone with Mum, telling her I needed surgery and that I would have a huge scar, but without the operation, I wouldn't make it. I was booked in for emergency surgery. Mum, Dad and James came into my room. I was still in emergency as they could not find me a bed, but I didn't care. Worrying or getting angry about having private health cover and not being in a private room was not part of my thinking. I didn't care where I slept as long as they made the pain go away.

The head nurse walked in with documentation and a gentle smile of controlled confidence. She proceeded to explain the situation. It looked like a twisted bowel, but they wouldn't know until they operated. The pump had not removed the contents of my bowel. She explained I had a tennis ball-sized mass in my bowel, which was twisted and starting to swell. She had more to say. Dad and James listened carefully.

The nurse explained the operation, a colostomy bag, which would be removed after ten weeks, and a redirection of stool matter. She asked for James' signature.

I scribbled my name somewhere on the page. James had to co-sign as he was my husband, and my signature was far from legible. As he signed, a tear ran down his cheek.

Just as I was ready to go into surgery, another patient was experiencing a complicated labour. The staff had to give her the operating room scheduled for me. Mum was fuming, and James was beside himself after hearing what could happen. The surgeon was angry; my time was running out; my blood would turn septic, which meant it would be toxic, and once that happened, the situation was perilous.

Finally, I was wheeled away. The last person I saw was James. We both smiled and released hands as I was being wheeled behind closed doors. I didn't understand what was happening, but I felt relaxed. The anaesthetic kicked in, and soon, I was drifting off into the blackness.

Two and a half hours later, my family came to the hospital together. Two sections of my bowel were twisted. I lost two feet of bowel. Staples and tape held me together. Some family members visited but didn't stay long. James was my last visitor. He was allowed to stay a little longer. I tried to look him in the eye, but all I could see were the tears in his eyes, which streamed down his face. He was in so much pain, and I wanted to comfort him, but all I could do was cry. Many years later, I wondered whether the tears were for me and the pain I was in or whether they were for himself. He had a sick wife who was on antidepressants, and now she had strange symptoms as well.

I made it through the night and was put in a private room next to the nurse's station on Level 6, where I remained in and out of consciousness for over a week. The smells and faint noises are my best recollections. I knew I couldn't talk; I could feel my eyes blink. I wasn't able to do anything. Wanting to go to the toilet was not even a thought. I was spaced out on drugs, but there was no pain. My family would visit and talk to each other; I could see them through my haze. I knew who they were, and when they touched me, it felt like I was being pulled or pushed. I was a stiff rag doll. I couldn't communicate, so they didn't talk much; they used touch instead, but I hoped that was an expression of love.

A pint-sized man was perched on my shoulder. I am convinced it was God. He was talking to himself, trying to decide on my future. Take her or leave her? It was like he was fighting with himself about what to do with me. I felt him and heard him every day. It was like one of those Kit-Kat ads. It went on for days: it was doing my head in. Finally, the silence was broken. I was able to speak. Eventually, I was talking, and I was up and about within twenty minutes.

My new nurse was a hard taskmaster. With James and her on either side of me, we went for my first walk in almost two and a half weeks. We walked up and down the corridor. I could feel something pulling as we walked. That walk was the worst. James was as gentle as possible, so I knew it wasn't something he was pulling. On the other side, the nurse was holding a bag and holding me. The bag the nurse held was attached to me, but I couldn't work out where and how it was attached. She kept lifting the bag higher and higher and walking quickly. It was like she was pulling me along. I had to work out where the tube was coming from and where it went. The pain was coming from my vagina. I had a catheter in, and I was scared that the nurse was pulling so hard she might pull it out, and there would be pain. I asked if I could carry the bag, and I felt better and more in control when she handed it over.

I worked out it was a catheter, and the catheter and I became best friends, but my bowel still wasn't behaving. I was past caring who saw me on the toilet.

My surgeon told me I could not go home until I had been to the toilet, so going to the toilet was a huge goal. He agreed to remove one of my tubes. I was keeping the catheter; he could have the nose tube. The catheter became part of many laughs with family and friends. I would ask them to please excuse me as I had to go to the bathroom. Everyone wanted to help me to the bathroom, and then I would say, "Thanks, but I've finished." The majority of the time, my visitors guessed I had a catheter, but the ones that didn't thought I had wet the bed. It was a joke I played on everyone. I had to entertain myself somehow. One night, James and I were watching TV, and my stomach started to make strange noises. We could see my stomach moving. I called a nurse, who informed us it was normal and that my bowel was working itself out, repositioning, and making room for itself. We watched it for a good ten minutes; it was like something out of this world, the noise, the movements and the weird feeling. We sat there in silence, watching. I was wondering if the surgeon had put something in there!

When I didn't have visitors, I would wake up very early and think about working harder on my marriage and putting in more effort. I thought about this every day.

My staples were the last items to be removed; actually, they didn't hurt as much as the catheter. The doctor agreed to let me go home to my parents as soon as I had gone to the toilet and passed faeces. My surgeon and the nurses kept asking if I had passed wind. I felt that was a little personal. I understood that passing wind is very important; it means the bowels are open and there is no blockage. I had been passing wind, and I had been to the toilet. I had been on solid food for about two days and doing well, so my surgeon gave me the all-clear and sent me to my parents.

I walked out of the hospital and started crying. Just being able to see, hear, touch and smell the air moving in the trees and feel the warm sun on my back was wonderful after weeks of medical procedures. The world was suddenly beautiful. I had always been an outdoor girl, and now it was like being a young girl again, out in the open, surrounded by earth, flowers, plants, trees, birds and blue sky above me.

8. **Holey Plum**

Because I couldn't do anything for myself after the operation and James had to go to work, we moved back in with my parents. I had to sit and rest, which meant everybody had to wait on me. I wasn't allowed to hold my niece. I had to be bathed by a family member. I quickly learned not to get too precious about privacy. Mum asked my cousin to bathe me as I could not do it myself. My cousin was studying nursing at university and was living with my parents. I was beyond skinny; my armpits were like deep holes. It was like bathing an old person.

James and I were given my parents' bedroom. They moved into the attic room. I was booked to see my surgeon on a Thursday. James didn't want to sleep with me in case he hurt me. He even tried sleeping on the floor so I could see him, but eventually, he moved into the bed. We were both scared, but I wanted him close. It was only four days till I was to see my surgeon. I wasn't even allowed to pick up my niece or change her nappy.

Watching yet another movie one afternoon, as there wasn't much I could do while recuperating, I was again aware of the sensation of the pint-sized friend sitting on my shoulder. He was back, thinking out loud about whether he had done the right thing or not. I got the feeling he still hadn't decided. Mum's friend was in the kitchen, and I overheard her say, "Melissa looks worse now than when she came home."

My visit to the surgeon was booked for the following Thursday, but by the Wednesday, I couldn't get out of bed. I just didn't have the energy. All I wanted was sto stay in one spot and sleep. Mum called the surgeon's office and got me an appointment that afternoon despite the surgery being busy. James came, as well. When the surgeon saw me, he asked my mother, "How many sick kids do you have?"

Mum explained what was happening, and he ushered us into his office. I was told to get on my knees. I remember James standing at my head, and his facial expression told me what was about to happen. My first rectal examination!

After that was over, I was told to dress and return to his office. I was weighed. Unbelievably, I weighed twenty-seven kilos, less than the average eight-year-old. The surgeon told us I had to be re-admitted to hospital immediately. I pleaded and pleaded with him not to send me back, but back I went.

While in hospital, I had the sensation that I could go to the toilet, and my Dad helped me to the toilet and sat with me while the rest of my family and James were in my room waiting. While I was on the toilet, the pain was indescribable. I was sure I had gone.

"Dad, can you look and wipe my bottom?"

All that trying had exhausted me. Dad had a look and reported that, unfortunately, I hadn't done anything. He had tears in his eyes. I asked my dad to let me go; I had had enough. I wanted to die. My Dad said he didn't want me to think of death. I started to scream. I wanted to die; I'd had enough. "Please, someone help me!" I screamed. "I can't take it anymore. Just let me go!"

A nurse came in and gave me a shot while I was still sitting on the toilet. She came in, located a spot she could get to on my bottom, stuck the needle in and left. James was standing at the entrance of the toilet and had heard everything; I felt sorry but had meant every word. I was almost at the bed when the injection started to work. Everyone helped get me into bed. Again, a nose tube was administered. The sister looked at me, then Mum and she was very hesitant.

Mum asked, "Is something wrong?"

"I have never had to do this to a young girl, only old people."

I just wanted to die; I didn't care. The nurse used the thickest nose tube possible. I couldn't speak; it was pressing on my vocal cords.

I had never taken much notice of those stories of the light in the tunnel when a person is under anaesthetic until it happened to me. I saw a light on my left. I felt alone, but someone was in the room with me besides my family. It wasn't just him this time; he wasn't alone. I wasn't scared. I was angry. Someone so powerful as he could decide. Then, the light appeared more potent, and I felt someone calling me.

"Melissa, walk with me."

The voice was very familiar. I was interested but had had enough. The light continued to shine, but not in an intense and blinding way, just in a warm and welcoming manner. I started to venture towards the light and look around. It was a long tunnel that looked like it had no end, but somehow, I could feel it went somewhere, somewhere special. Then I saw my Nanny.

"I love you, but it's not your time; you must go back."

"The man behind you. Is that him?"

"Go back, do not touch me, or you will not be able to return."

"He, God, has been playing with me. I can't take much more. How do I know what he wants from me?"

"God wants you to live, but your recovery will not be easy, and there is a lot more pain and suffering to come."

She looked so beautiful and peaceful.

"Turn around and go now! DO NOT LOOK BACK!"

I could feel her love, her warmth, even though we were not touching. She winked and smiled. I felt James' hand holding me tight, and I could hear him crying. I had to be with him. I turned around and ran back to James. James told me what the surgeon had said when I woke. He explained that due to my weight, it was not possible to reopen the bowel and give me another colostomy bag. According to the surgeon, I would not be able to handle the anaesthetic due to my size. He told my parents that I would not live through that night, and he suggested they call their priest. James was the last to leave; we never spoke about how he was feeling. Even now, I wish I knew. Everyone else had left knowing my fate and wondering whether this could be the last time they saw me. I will never know how they felt. I can only imagine. I was back in my bed, alone and looking to make a deal. My demands were straightforward and direct. These were my terms. If I woke up in the morning, meaning I was still here, *He* was not allowed to interfere with my recovery. I was very serious and made sure we both understood.

That night was tough; the nose tube was a problem. I would sleep and then wake up, and my first thought would be that I was still here, but he still had *time*. Sometimes, I would lie there and wonder what time it was. At one stage, I lay and listened to the sounds of the machine, the machine that was connected through my nose tube into my stomach, which was trying to remove the unwanted elements from my stomach. I listened to the rhythm of the machine going up and down, up and down. At times, the nurses would wake me when they were doing their observations. It was the longest night ever.

Morning came, and I remember waking up and realising I was still in the land of the living. I looked up and said, "OK. So, we agree. I am going to get better." I couldn't wait for James to arrive; I guess by the look of him, he had had no sleep, waiting for that final call, the one that would have changed his life forever. He walked into my room with his brother, not knowing what to expect. I tried to smile. To speak, I had to push against my throat with at least three fingers so I could get something out. It hurt, so I didn't do it often. James and his brother took me downstairs, where I was scheduled for another x-ray. Our families were both there.

I went for an x-ray, which was a horrible experience as I could taste the dye and kept coughing against the tube.

The x-ray technician could see I was distressed and asked if I wanted someone with me as it would be a while before they were ready, and the dye settled. I asked for my husband. Not only was I sick, but they thought I was losing my mind. Husband? They went back and looked at my paperwork. They thought I was about twelve years old and couldn't believe I was almost twenty-five. James came in just in time to be with me when I needed to go to the toilet. This time, something happened. I held James' hand and pushed through the pain. I gave birth to my blockage! I couldn't believe it. James was very proud of me and couldn't wait to tell the others. I can laugh about that proud moment now!

I returned to have my x-ray, which showed no blockage as I had just released it. The nurse took me to the ICU and placed me on a TPN drip. The bed was tipped upwards, so my head was close to the floor. All the blood ran to my upper body, and it was not good for my head. TPN is used for patients who cannot or should not get nutrition through eating. TPN may include a combination of sugar and carbohydrates (for energy), proteins (for muscle strength), lipids (fat), electrolytes, and trace elements. The solution may contain all or some of these substances, depending on a person's condition.

The drip was placed through my chest into my main artery. I had to stay like that until the portable X-ray machine arrived to make sure it was in the right place and not in my heart. As soon as it was confirmed to be in the right artery, the surgeon in his all-greens and mask sewed it in tighter and put my bed back up.

I remember thinking he was pretty good-looking and would be great for Amanda.

I was now totally over the nose tube; I couldn't breathe properly and couldn't talk. Enough was enough. I told her if she wasn't going to do it, I would do it myself. She quickly ran off to call my surgeon again.

When she returned, she told me that the surgeon had said that if I removed the nose tube, I would most probably die as it was keeping me alive. Bullshit, I told them. I was keeping myself alive because of my self-talk and my bargain with God. I started undoing the tape on my nose. My Mum was screaming. James was crying and begging me not to do it, and my boss, Derek, was amazed. Derek knew I was a determined woman, but he hadn't expected to see that.

Mum was still screaming, telling me I would die if I removed it as it was keeping me alive. By that stage, I didn't care if I did die; I was over it, the pain, the discomfit, and the inability to swallow. Finally, the tape was undone, and I started pulling the tube out of my nose. It was very long. Eventually, my favourite nurse came in, stood at the end of my bed, and kept pulling the tube. It took a while to pull out the entire tube. The relief was instant. I was so grateful; I could swallow, breathe and talk. Mum looked angry, but I didn't care. I was free of that tube. It left a dent in my nose.

My family visited when they could. James was amazing. He was at work by 6 am, worked a long day, and then was at my bedside until the staff asked him to leave. He was living with my parents so that he could be closer to me.

At times in the day, I would stare at my TPN line and watch the fats and oils drip into my system. They took the TPN tube out after ten days. I was still going to be there for a while as I could not go to the toilet.

One afternoon, my Mum and Amanda came with me to the bathroom. Privacy had long gone out the window. I was still extremely thin, so Amanda had to keep hold of me. We kept laughing as I tried to go to the toilet. I thought I had something for that toilet bowl. Manda kept checking, but there wasn't anything. That just made them laugh more. Laughing was not for me as it hurt too much. Trying to pass anything on the toilet was very tiring. I was now able to wipe myself, but I honestly didn't care who wiped me or saw me naked. I was past all that. When I was alone, I couldn't reach around to do up the ties on the back of my hospital gown, so everyone in the ICU got a daily view of my behind. I was beyond caring.

I had a lot of visitors and could see the parking lot from the window. I watched people coming and going.

I finally went to the toilet, which was a considerable feat. It felt like I had just done ten rounds with Mike Tyson. It might sound ludicrous, but anyone who has suffered from severe constipation or bowel problems will understand what a relief it is when it finally happens! All the nurses and doctors cheered, as did the other ICU patients. Now, it was time to fatten me up. Tegan brought in cheeseburgers and a chocolate thick shake. Food I would never eat. I don't call McDonald's food. Nil by mouth, TPN and hospital food was forgotten as I devoured a hamburger. It was fattening and heavenly.

After another two weeks, I was allowed to leave the hospital. It had almost been six weeks.

I said good-bye to all my nurses. I was still very sore but happy that I wasn't leaving in a wheelchair but using my legs. I was delighted to be in a car going home and not on a slab going to the morgue. The feeling of fresh air on my face and the smells of the trees when I stepped outside were amazing. I was lost in that moment and loved it.

I was thrilled to be out of hospital. If there was one thing I would never forget, it was the experience of seeing my Nanny. I believe that what had happened was a near-death experience. People who have had these experiences often report that their senses are heightened after the event. Nothing like that happened to me. I didn't feel that something profound, something that would change my life forever, had occurred. It was simply that my Nanny came from heaven to tell me that it was not my time.

I'd known the recovery was something that I could not rush. It would be a long and challenging process and something I couldn't control. I had a few tremors in my arms and legs while I was recovering, but I put it down to the effects of anaesthetic and was too tired to think much about it.

During my follow-up visit with the bowel surgeon, I hardly had a chance to get a word. The surgeon told me that the operation had been successful and that I should have no more problems. I told him I was feeling fine. My mother dismissed what I was saying with a wave of her hand and told the surgeon that, in her opinion, I was suffering from coeliac disease. The surgeon told her that there was no evidence that I had coeliac. She insisted that I had it.

"Melissa would probably benefit from a gluten-free diet, yes, but she does *not* suffer from coeliac."

It was embarrassing. My mother was arguing with a surgeon as if she had more knowledge than he did. I tried to say something, but my mother overrode me. The surgeon looked decidedly unimpressed. It was almost as though she desperately wanted me to have the condition. I didn't understand it, but put it down to one of her odd displays.

In 2001, after my bowel operation, I started to experience similar sensations to those I had felt before and during the time of my wedding. I was twenty-six years old. When I experienced strange phenomena back in 1998, I put it down to the stress of the wedding. Now, I put them down to the effects of the anaesthetic.

Sometimes, I'd look at cars and couldn't tell whether they were moving or stationary. It was totally weird. This sensation was happening more regularly. One morning, I was standing in my parents' kitchen, waiting for the kettle to boil, when my mother and brother walked in from the backyard. Andrew stopped Mum and just stood watching me. His mouth fell open, and his eyes welled up. Mum asked him what was wrong.

"Mum, something's wrong with Melissa."

Mum looked at me and noticed I was watching the TV, but my head was going up and down very quickly. *Days of Our Lives* was on the television. It was a scene between John Black and Marlana. I didn't worry too much about it as I thought it was the leftover effects of the anaesthetic from my operation. I was trying to make the picture on the screen stay still, but it wouldn't, so the best way for me to follow it was to move with it, which is why I was moving my head up and down. All I could see was feet and hair, but not much in between on the screen.

"What's she doing?"

"She thinks something's moving, and she's trying to follow it, but nothing's moving. I think her brain's seeing it differently."

"Is that bad?"

"Yes, very."

A battery of tests followed. I was sent for an immediate cat scan of my head and brain. I didn't process what was happening; it was yet another test, and the thought of more tests made me feel sick. In addition to that, I was still processing my bowel operation, and my mind couldn't cope with this new round of tests.

I wanted fresh air, birds, grass, and sun, not doctors' offices.

Back at the doctor's office, Mum sat close to the doctor, and I sat in a single chair. The doctor was reading the report and looking at the scans. The office was once a bedroom in an old federation house; it was large and dark, and I felt it had housed a lot of negative conversation. The doctor reached for Mum's hand and took a deep breath. It was not looking good. She said something about knowing each other for a long time and the need to be honest.

'I've booked Melissa in to see the number one neurologist, as I believe after reading the report, looking at her scans and tests that Melissa has a brain tumour."

It was one of those moments when it didn't register straight away. Mum started to cry while my thoughts whirled.

Come on, God, are you serious? Haven't I had enough? Didn't you and I make a deal?

The doctor arranged for additional tests at the balance clinic across from Royal Prince Alfred Hospital, which led to more tests, and then I still had to wait another two weeks. Being booked in to see the number one neurologist in Sydney meant only two things to me: one – I would get the best care and medical advice, or two – my diagnosis was so serious, he or she was my one and only chance.

I heard my mother on the phone to her friends.

"What have I done to deserve this? Now, there's a new illness. Do I ever get a break from this?"

We had booked our family holiday before this latest medical news and still went. I used the time as an opportunity to focus on different things. My looming diagnosis was always in the back of my mind, even on holidays. Nothing made the two weeks pass any faster. That grey cloud put a damper on everything, no matter how much we tried not to think about what was coming next.

"Strip down to just underpants, take all jewellery off and put on that very attractive medical gown, then sit and wait."

That was my introduction to MRI scans and the new world in which I was about to participate. I was ushered into another room, which housed one crazy-sized machine. The staff told me to get up on the bed, and they gave me earplugs and what looked like construction headphones. They told me that the bed would slide into a tunnel. I had to lie down and not move. I would hear noises but was told not to react. My heart was pounding, I was sweating, and then I was alone, and the noises started.

A jackhammer, chimes, sirens, bells, alarms, nothing and then it started again. Finally, I heard the door open and was told I could get up and dress. My scans would be sent to the neurologist.

On Thursday, 25 January 2001, I sat in a waiting room like most waiting rooms: chairs against both sides of the walls, magazines on a low table, bland paint, a reception desk and a filing cabinet behind it. My mother and James were with me. The faces in these waiting rooms are also the same, plastered with fear and dread – the unknown. There are usually at least two other strangers waiting with you; the person waiting before you as the doctor is always running late and the one booked in after you. There is always a receptionist whose face gives nothing away. Always professional. They are used to people crying. It was impossible to read the magazines on the low table if I had wanted to. In these moments, concentration on anything but the test result is out of the question. Mum and James sat, saying nothing.

Sitting there, I knew the man behind that door at the end of the corridor had seen my results already. He knew my future. I didn't. My head was spinning with questions: Are the results good or bad? What if they're bad? What does it mean if they're bad? How is this going to affect my future? Do I even have a future? Aren't some tumours benign? Are you going to tell me that you can cut it out, whatever it is? All right, I'm so over hospitals, but I'm ready for another operation if it means I'll be well. I thought about all those people who had walked from the waiting area down the corridor and into his office to face their future. In a few moments, their lives could change forever. So could mine.

"Please, let it be something that can be fixed! Please. Please. Please!"

I was pleading with the universe, with God, with my own body, with anything that might have the power to make sure that it was something minor that had a solution.

Mum was tugging at my arm to get up as my name had been called. So lost in my own thoughts, I hadn't heard. We walked the short walk into the office. I looked at the doctor's face, trying to read it. He asked us to sit. I liked his manner and felt comfortable with him, but I was utterly unprepared for what he had to say next. He was matter-of-fact but gentle. He took a deep breath and leaned forward.

"Melissa, what you have is a progressive degeneration of the cerebellum, what we call Cerebral Atrophy."

He could see from our facial expressions we didn't understand. "Cerebral what?" I asked.

"Cerebral Atrophy means that there is shrinkage of the brain tissue."

I understood the words. Shrinkage. Brain Tissue. I still didn't understand what it meant for me.

"What? My brain is getting smaller? I don't understand. What does it do?"

The doctor produced my MRI scans and proceeded to explain to me what was happening.

Cerebral Atrophy is a brain disease. The cells in my cerebellum were decreasing in size, which was usually the result of a loss of cytoplasmic proteins. When the brain becomes atrophied, the connections between the brain and the neurons that keep it connected become smaller. The atrophy could affect the whole brain or parts of the brain, which means that certain functions controlled by those parts are affected. We have two cerebral hemispheres, the right and the left. The right hemisphere controls and processes signals from the left side of the body, while the left hemisphere controls and processes signals from the right side of the body. The doctor also spoke about the connection between the brain and the bowel. My mother started to look very uncomfortable. I could not imagine what the two areas of my brain looked like. He explained it in another way.

"Imagine two plums ready to eat, all ripe and juicy. Melissa's plum on the left-hand side is good to eat, but the one on the right has holes in it, so it's not good to eat. So, the right one will wither up because it has been eaten into by the worm."

"Ok, then, great. I am like a bad piece of fruit."

"I have been very matter-of-fact because you need to understand what you have is a very serious disease."

"What's my future looking like then?"

The doctor leaned forward again. He could read the fear in my eyes. He spoke very gently.

"There is a high chance you will be in a wheelchair by the end of this year."

I didn't have time to feel anything or say anything as Mum started up, the creeping hysteria in her voice growing louder and louder.

"Don't blame me for this, as it certainly has nothing to do with me! It must come from her father's side. It's his fault. It's something in his genes!"

The doctor was clearly shocked and didn't know who to look at next. James and I looked at each other. Blaming someone was not the answer; dealing with the situation was. There was an awkward silence. The doctor scribbled on his notepad. He looked up, and the expression on his face was not hard to read. Did her mother really just say that?

I knew the reason why my mother had reacted in the way she did. On Mum's side of the family, they all had some medical condition to do with the stomach and bowels. Mum was fond of deflecting blame away from her side of the family. Still, her defensive attitude and outburst when I needed her to be calm and rational and focus on what I needed was too much to handle in the doctor's office. It didn't surprise me that my mother had said this. I was used to hearing how much of a burden I was, but I was astounded that she had picked this moment to speak about blame.

"It's not about who to blame," I said. "Let's just listen to what the doctor is saying so we can understand what this means."

My mother looked at me. She was not impressed. Her face hardened.

"Oh, my God," I said. "Can we please not get into whose fault it was? For Christ's sake, it doesn't matter. Can we just focus on what I've just been told and listen?"

I wanted James to back me up, but he stayed silent (of course.) This was the most devastating moment in my life, and he couldn't support me. My mind and body were screaming internally. Why didn't he say something? What is wrong with you? I wanted to scream. Say something. Back me up, for God's sake, but he said nothing. The doctor suggested we bring the focus back to understanding what we'd just been told and what the next steps would be. He explained that we still don't know enough about the causes. Infections of the brain can cause it, but research is still ongoing. He went on to explain that one of my legs was already affected. This now made sense.

"Is this what's causing my legs to shake sometimes?"

The doctor nodded. He explained the symptoms of the disease, which include seizures, convulsions or repetitive movements of the limbs. He went on to explain the causes of cerebral atrophy: aging generally shrinks the brain and we all lose brain volume as we age. The cells decline the older we get. Brain injury, disease and stroke are other factors that cause the disease. Brain disorders such as Huntington's, Alzheimer's, corticobasal and progressive supranuclear palsy can cause it as well. Stroke or trauma can obstruct blood flow to the brain and starve it of oxygen, leading to atrophy. A lack of vitamin B12 and too much alcohol can also bring about atrophy.

"I will not allow myself to be in a wheelchair. So what do we start doing to stop this from happening?"

The doctor paused before he spoke.

"You have all had a lot to take in, so let's leave it at this for today, but we need to make another appointment later this week to arrange some more tests."

I could tell that the doctor didn't want to get into a discussion with me about my determination not to be in a wheelchair by year's end. He'd doubtless seen hundreds of patients in his career who'd probably responded the same way I had just done. He'd probably put it down to another patient in denial. Well, I wasn't like most patients, I told myself.

9. **Square Metres**

James went back to work that day. I was hoping he would take the rest of the day off, but I knew he would put work first. It didn't surprise me. When we got home, my mother raved all afternoon about how the bad genes were on my father's side. She went on and on about it so much that I went into another room. At night, my mother was still going on about how it was my Dad's side. My Dad wasn't home, and if he had been there, there would have been no way she would have carried on like that. My sister popped around with my favourite ice-cream. It was her way of saying that she was there for me.

When James got home from work, he didn't talk about the diagnosis at all that night. I think he went into denial. It was business as usual. The elephant in the room was huge, and from that point on, I knew that I was on my own. One night, not long after my diagnosis, my parents spoke to James by himself. They told James that they did not expect him to hold to his marriage vows and that he could just walk away and there would be no hard feelings. She'll be in a wheelchair by the end of the year, they told him. There's no future for you, they said.

Later that night, when we were home, I asked James about his conversation with my parents. He told me. I was angry and hurt. Nobody had bothered to ask about what I wanted. I was still going to work and earning more than any of them, was competent and organised and was not going to be in a wheelchair. How dare they suggest that my husband leave me. I wasn't invited to be part of that conversation, and any discussion about my future with my husband should have been between him and me. Although I was terribly hurt, I didn't confront my parents.

Over the next few months, because I wasn't asking anyone to do anything extra and because nothing had changed since my diagnosis, I think everyone believed that I was doing all right. Since I had been told the bad news, the only symptom that I was experiencing was the sensation that stationary things were moving, like cars and some headaches. A lot of things didn't change at all, and because of that, I lulled myself into thinking that I could defeat the illness by sheer will power, exercise and diet. I lived in a bubble of determination.

I was still under the delusion that I wouldn't succumb to the symptoms of my illness until the morning when I had my first fall in late April 2001. James was in another room, playing a computer game. I was going to lie down when I approached the bed, and suddenly, my legs gave way beneath me. I fell, landing on the hard floor. I couldn't get up, so I yelled out for James to help me. I don't know if he could hear me properly because he answered that he was busy landing a plane on a computer game. Finally, he came into the room, but by then, I had already hoisted myself up. Again, my thought was I would have to deal with this on my own. It was then that I had my first real panicked thoughts about my disease.

"Oh, shit," I said to myself. *What just happened? What is happening to me?*

I was shocked. That night, as I lay in bed, two streams of competing thoughts looped around in my head. There was the tough, focused person whose characteristics and determination saw her climbing up in her career. Then, there was the terrified, shell-shocked woman looking into a future that was too awful to contemplate.

What would happen to me? Would I be able to keep on working? What about my marriage, and could I still have children? I lay awake, lurching from one position to another. Anxiety rose inside me. Who would take care of me? James was proving to be useless, so I had to gear myself up to tackle my new situation alone. I needed to be independent. I simply couldn't rely on him. What about all the medical bills? What's going to happen next? Will I wake up tomorrow, and this disease will be worse? I tossed and turned all night.

I was not going to be in a wheelchair by the end of the year. I would do everything to prevent that from happening and start on the rounds of health practitioners. I would do whatever it took. I would exercise, do weights, and get a personal trainer. It was difficult at times to stay focused and not let negativity get in the way. I started on the rounds of doctors, surgeons, neurologists and other health practitioners. Again, I was not allowed to do anything, so I spent six months at my parents' house and then four months with James' parents. I didn't properly process what the doctor told me because I was too busy keeping busy.

I processed it on an intellectual level but not on an emotional one. There were two reasons for this. Firstly, I suppressed it. Denial is natural; it's your brain's way of protecting you from information that's just too hard to bear. Secondly, not only was I trying to manage my own illness, but I was managing my mother and my husband, who were not helpful at all. Her blame game and his ineptitude in not standing up for me were exhausting. Anyone would think they were the ones with a life-threatening illness. They were both looking for sympathy, but neither of them was capable of supporting me constructively. My mother was absorbed in herself. She only saw events in relation to how they affected her. Her dramatic posturing got me down. She wanted the world to see how much she was suffering from having such an ill daughter. James, who I wanted to be strong for me, was anything but. I had more resourcefulness and strength than both of them put together.

"Don't get fixated" was James' contribution to my determination to get better. I didn't take much notice of that comment. He knew that whatever I did, I would do it one hundred per cent. And there lay the unfairness. For the first time in my life, I had found something at which I excelled. My career was my lifeline to better self-esteem and a good lifestyle. It countered all the negative comments that had been bashed into my head by my mother. When I was at work, I was invincible. Would all this be taken away? I definitely would be just as 'fixated' with getting better as I was at work. I was going to give it one hundred per cent. My family took their usual holiday together soon after that in Foster.

I pushed my emotions down, not wanting to face the reality that my life would change. I talked to my disease. It helped me manage the despair and anger that would creep over me.

"I'll deal with you later," I told my disease. "Right now, I'm dealing with other people who aren't dealing with it either."

I got through that holiday by pretending that everything was all right. "Fuck you, Cerebral Atrophy. This isn't going to happen. No way."

"You can't escape me, Melissa. I'm coming for you."

"Piss off! Wheelchair? Who are you kidding? I'm gonna beat you, CA!"

"You heard the doctor. And you don't know which part of your body will start falling apart next. I'll decide that, Melissa, because I'm in control of you now."

"Just piss off, all right? I'm stronger than you think I am. I'm not useless. I'm not stupid. I'm not all those things Mum says I am. I have no idea why she says that when she can see where I've got so far with my career. I'm going to show everybody. CA, *you will not stop me*!"

As the months passed, I tried to deal with the news by throwing myself into work. I was working as a leasing agent for several different companies in Sydney. Deep down inside, there was an underlying thought that lay at the bottom of my consciousness: I deserved this disease. It was yet another layer of sickness that had been imposed on me by fate, God, the universe or whatever controlled our destinies. My mother had always told me that I was a bad person and so I thought having the disease was in proportion to my degree of wickedness. It never occurred to me to think about it any differently. I didn't voice these thoughts to anybody. I kept them to myself. I pushed them down, but they never went away. The belief that I was given this disease as punishment was always lurking there. Even though I never understood why I was so bad, the perception that I was bad was ingrained, so much so that it became just as much an explanation for my disease as the pure medical facts put before me.

I kept working, and, looking back, I didn't think I was that badly affected. Then, small changes started to take place that had enormous consequences. One morning at work, I found I was having trouble working out square metres for a new retail space in one of the centres I was managing. I tried several times but just couldn't get it right. Coffee, that's what I need, I thought. It made no difference. I decided to leave it till the next day. The next day, however, was even worse. Not only couldn't I do the maths, but I also couldn't work out the right tenancy mix, and I couldn't understand the contracts, all things that were second nature to me. That skill was gone, and it happened over a few days. As the weeks went by, I was having trouble retaining information. It was a shock. I was devastated. I no longer controlled my destiny. I couldn't get my head around that. I kept talking to my illness, especially whenever I found that suddenly I wasn't able to do certain things anymore.

"Ok, disease, you've won that one. I can't do maths anymore, but you're not winning the next round coz I'm fighting you."

A few weeks would go by, and suddenly, I wasn't able to do certain things anymore. I still kept to my ritual of talking to the disease.

"Right, I can't read the contracts, but I can still talk to the clients and work on other ways to get all the stuff done, so there, piss off, CA."

"Ok, new tenancy contracts – someone else can do those bits, and I'll still do the major work on the rest of the program, so get stuffed; I'm onto it."

These conversations helped alleviate my anxiety about my future. I can still do this. I can still do this. I can.

The doctor was right. I did, indeed, have a lot to take in. I had a battery of tests to face in the coming weeks, which would give the doctors more information about what was happening in my brain and body. I had a lumbar puncture soon after.

I had to toughen up very quickly as some of the tests were painful. The worst for me was the muscle biopsy. This procedure is done by removing a small tissue sample so doctors can determine whether there is an infection or disease in the muscles. No anaesthetic is given because the muscle has to be alive when the sample is taken. I believe the procedure has changed since I had it. I cried during this procedure. I had to sign a document allowing them to take samples from two places on my body: my right arm and leg. The surgeon came in and put on some classical music, which was designed to keep the patient calm, I supposed. I wasn't calm at all. The pain was incredible. After the arm was done, I told him I couldn't endure another one. The surgeon explained that one sample wasn't enough, and if I didn't agree to the next one, the first one would have been in vain.

"All right," I said. "But could I have some heavy metal music on?"

The nurse went out and returned to say there was no heavy metal music. When it was finished, I burst into tears. It was a barbaric test. I knew I would have many more tests to come, so I had to get used to being poked and prodded and hurt.

The next test was not painful. It was a sweat test, which measures the amount of chloride excreted during sweating. This test is done to screen for cystic fibrosis. I had to wear old clothing, especially underwear, and not wear anything white. I was instructed to bring a clean set of clothing as I had to shower after the test. The staff rubbed me down with a product like talcum powder. This powder allows the sweat to turn purple. I was then placed inside a huge plastic box with a heater. A timer started when I started to sweat. I had to stay in the box for two hours. After emerging from the box, the staff took photographs of my body. I took a shower, but the purple did not come completely off for a few days.

I didn't know at the time that the test was to examine for cystic fibrosis. If I had known that's what the test was for, I would have completely lost it. I would have thought: Do you think I have something else? Really? On top of what I already have? I found out later. Fortunately, after the test, the staff told me I had sweated in all the right spots, and nothing sinister had shown up. I was very grateful and relieved.

In the following years, I would have blood tests, nerve conduction tests, MRIs, brain scans, laparoscopies, colonoscopies, ultrasounds, CAT scans, imaging injections and many more tests, so I had to come to terms with the fact that this would be a part of my life. It was tedious, exhausting and sometimes painful but I toughened up quickly.

Added to the stress of tests and the uncertainty of what I was facing, I had the added stress of trying to please my mother when nothing I did seemed to be right and trying to cope with James, who was increasingly behaving like a child. He was falling apart and cried constantly. He cried because of my illness. He cried because he wasn't enjoying the job he was doing. I became very frustrated with him because he couldn't stand up for himself with specific companies he was working for at the time. He wouldn't ask for a pay rise. He just seemed so weak. When I questioned him about why he couldn't stand up for himself regarding a pay increase, he told me that it was more important to enjoy your job than worry about money. The only problem with that sentiment was that if he were a single guy, then yes, I would have agreed. But he was in a relationship; we had a future to plan, a mortgage, children perhaps, all the things that go with family life. I wanted the other man, my soulmate, and I increasingly thought about him as living with James was becoming more and more difficult.

My frustration with that situation was also because James was very talented. However, he was going to waste his talents if he didn't start toughening up at home and at work. I understood that he was devastated about my illness, but I needed him to be strong for me, to show support, to talk through the issues that we were facing. We needed to talk about everything because everything was going to change. Being emotionally strong for both of us was not only exhausting but unreasonable.

I often asked him why he couldn't be more assertive, but he couldn't give me a satisfactory answer. Intimacy between us had stopped some time ago. I loved him but I was frustrated, tired and very confused. We seemed to be constantly fighting, and he was always defending my mother. I didn't understand why he wasn't defending his wife against the negative comments from his mother-in-law. I couldn't understand why he was the one crying when I was the one with the terrible prognosis. I was focusing on how to keep going while he was doing anything but. I had no one to rely on but myself. I know James was raised to respect elders, but staying silent when his mother-in-law commented negatively about his wife was not good enough. I expected more.

I was accustomed to my mother's negative comments, and although they hurt me, I never challenged them. I still tried to please her. One evening, we had to go to a family function that was held at a club not far from where James and I lived. I wore what I thought was an appropriate outfit for the occasion, but when my mother saw me, she looked me up and down.

"I didn't think you'd wear that," she said and went on to describe what she thought I should be wearing.

"I can go home and get changed," I said. "It's only around the corner." My mother just rolled her eyes and sighed.

Although I was sick, I was determined to overcome the obstacles that were holding me back. I decided to leave the national role and start my own consulting business in 2001. I asked James to help me make the decision, but he kept saying it was totally up to me. I understood he didn't want me to blame him if it didn't work out. We both knew I would have. I had been with the other company for six years, but I knew I had the skills to head up a company and be an independent businesswoman. I believed it would allow me more time to devote to personal things. Be home more and not so much travelling. I realised pretty soon that working for myself did not allow me more time at all. I was travelling continuously. I would wake up in a hotel and wonder which state I was in and where I was off to that day. It was intense.

I had some contacts, and I worked hard to establish a well-run organisation. Before long, I had enough work and employed James as well. That year, 2001, I worked on the *Vanilla Sky* premiere event. Tom Cruise and Penelope Cruz had come to Australia to promote the film, and there was much to do. I was in charge of the red carpet, and I opened the doors of the limousines. I got to meet Tom Cruise and look after him on the night. I didn't fawn over the celebrities; I was there to do a job, and the company was impressed with my attitude.

My mother and sisters saw me on television.

"How come you were near the celebrities?" they asked. They looked at me like I was some sort of alien they didn't recognise.

"Just doing my job," I said.

My mother did her usual thing of feigning total surprise that her 'dumb' daughter got a job looking after someone famous.

"What's Tom Cruise like?" my sister asked.

"He's shorter than me," I replied and left the room.

The *Vanilla Sky* event led me to work at Tropfest. Tropfest was a huge job. With shopping centre events and things like Tropfest, I was working two months ahead as there was so much to do before the event. Firstly, there are things to organise for the workers of the events company itself. The workers are there on site for some time before the night. I had to organise portaloos for the staff, organise cleaners, bar staff, and waiters, as well as the VIP area, the green room, the marquee, the red carpet, a separate portaloo area for the VIPs and also put names on seats at the front for the important guests. Usually, I was sent information about who was coming. Before I started working for Tropfest, the VIP marquee was a plain white tent. I sourced a marquee with a clear, thick plastic roof so the guests inside could look up and see the stars. They still use a clear marquee up to the present day, and I feel proud of instituting this. Even though I was sick, I kept it to myself and ploughed through. One afternoon, I went up on the cherry-picker and helped put up banners. I wanted to walk on the scaffolding, but I wasn't allowed. I went on to do Tropfest for a few years.

Every year, Tropfest has a theme that requires that a particular object be included in every film submitted. That year, the object that had to be included was a match. There was a giant match kept in a box, which was placed on the lounge when interviews were being done. When the match arrived, I ran across and collected it and returned to where it was to be put. I opened the box, and there was nothing inside. I felt sick but looked at the end of the box only to see it was open. I retraced my steps, found the match on the grass, and breathed a sigh of relief. It wouldn't have looked good if the themed object of the night went missing.

Because Tropfest was held in a part of the Botanical Gardens, I got to meet one of the teams in charge of the gardens, and he asked me to send him some information with a reference. They needed a person to do a big event – New Year's Eve.

My business was taking off, and over the next few years, I worked hard to ensure that it was a solidly run company with total professionalism. I was good at liaising with the management of celebrities and ensuring that everything was running smoothly for their appearances. I worked with international actors, athletes, and musical artists. I knew their food preferences and other pieces of information that would hopefully ensure there were no surprises on the day. Everything had to be checked and double-checked.

I worked with Boyz II Men, Manpower, CBD, Dannii Minogue, The Fugees, The American Presidents, LeeAnn Rimes, Harry C, Marcia Hines, Human Nature and Pink. Boyz II Men was a particularly memorable time. At the time, they were at the peak of their career. I ordered the required barricading and security, but the number of people who turned out to see them was beyond what anyone could have imagined, and there was the danger of a crowd crush, so I had to think quickly. There was no way James could have done that type of work. It would have been totally out of his league. My friends were in awe that I was working with such famous names, but I didn't let that affect my professional obligations. I wasn't there to make friends with celebrities. My job came first, and my reputation in the industry did as well.

2003 was a busy year. I was climbing up in my career, but nobody in my family ever commented on how well I was doing. One afternoon, I went into my brother's bedroom, and he was talking with his girlfriend on the bed. Just as I entered the room, I heard him comment that I made the most money in the family. I knew that my family was in awe of this, but it was like a taboo subject. I wished they'd stop being so surprised that I had talents.

While I was working, I was trying to deal with the way James was handling my illness. I didn't think he was dealing with it very well at all. I understood it was difficult, but I didn't need the extra stress of trying to manage *him* while trying to manage myself. A job offer came up in Melbourne that would last a year. I couldn't do it. I had three contracts in Sydney and ongoing appointments with specialists. I was stretched to the limit in every way. I encouraged James to move to Melbourne. I would come down to Melbourne when I could. I was so focused on just getting through day-to-day with my illness that I didn't have time to worry about him. He was an adult, but it was like dealing with a child. I had enough to do just dealing with myself. This period of working in different cities would give me time to do what I needed to do to control my illness and get my head around how I was going to manage it long-term. It would give James a chance as well to process how my condition was going to affect our marriage and to think of ways that we could handle it together. I hoped that he would man-up a bit. I couldn't be strong for both of us. It was taking all my energy to stay working and deal with my health. James agreed to take the job in Melbourne.

As soon as it was possible, I started with a chiropractor, Hugh, who was James' brother. It was my first appointment since my bowel resection. I was undergoing a massage from a female masseuse and dressed only in underpants but covered by a towel when suddenly she said something that made me glad I was lying down.

"How strange is this?" she said, "We've both slept with the same guy!"

I realised who she was – James' ex-girlfriend. Her hands were on my body; I was in a vulnerable position and now felt totally powerless. A massage is somewhat of an intimate and personal experience and should be with someone you feel you can trust. I had a massive scar on my body and felt exposed as it was. I felt violated and sick.

When I arrived home, I got stuck into James. He didn't see my point. "She lost her job when Ansett airlines collapsed, and she needed a job."

"And you think it perfectly all right that you suggest your brother's business where your ex-girlfriend works and not tell me first? It would have been nice to have been told and then have the option of going or not going. And you think it's perfectly fine that she works on my body? And it's perfectly all right for her to say what she said? It's *totally unprofessional,* for a start. It's a breach of privacy. She shouldn't be discussing things like that with clients. It's completely unethical. People can get sacked for that sort of thing."

He still didn't see my point of view.

Hugh and James honestly believed I would not have a problem with it. I was angry. They had known all along. They had no idea how humiliating it had been to have had an ex-girlfriend massaging me and making inappropriate comments while touching me. I don't know how I got through that massage without bursting into tears. Even knowing she was in the building was too much. When that woman entered the room, she knew who I was. Hugh's wife, the receptionist, hadn't said anything either. If I had known and had had a choice, I'd never have gone for that appointment. I couldn't believe that James had subjected me to that. I never went back to that building ever again. Yet it seemed that I couldn't get rid of her. Soon after, I had a hair appointment, and there she was, working at the reception desk. Was she following me? She always asked me about James as if they were close friends. I wasn't rude but straightforward and only used one-answer responses.

James did not understand why I felt angry about this woman. I couldn't understand how he couldn't understand. I kept it down, but I was furious.

One night, when James and I were asking each other about what we had eaten for lunch that day, James casually told me that he had had lunch with his ex-girlfriend, the masseur who had so upset me. She just needed to talk to someone, he told me.

"Why you?" I asked.

"She's having problems with her husband."

"So, she picks *my* husband to talk to?"

I felt betrayed. James had told me at the beginning of our relationship that he believed it was unfair and disrespectful of a current partner to keep in contact with ex-partners. It's not right, he told me. What was in the past should stay there, he believed. Despite being angry about the lunch, I still trusted him, so James moved to Melbourne. I had done all the hard work, negotiated the contract, the living conditions, the salary, everything. James stepped into a good job, a lovely apartment and a good salary. My first visit to Melbourne didn't quite go as I had planned. We argued over his constant reference to Tanya, a girl who worked with him. He told me that the woman he had the most interaction with at the company was an older woman named Elizabeth.

"Then why are you always talking about Tanya? If you have so much interaction with Elizabeth, then why aren't I hearing more about her?"

I wasn't suspicious. I was irritated and had much more on my mind than wondering about Tanya. Perhaps if I hadn't been dealing with a serious illness, my intuitive faculties might have been sharper. I was convinced that James would never do anything 'like that.'

The next time I decided to fly and see my husband, I didn't tell anyone. I thought I would surprise him. I was flying down on a Friday evening and was returning on Sunday evening. When I got off the plane, I hailed a taxi and arrived at the place where James was staying. As I arrived, I saw James' car pulling out of the driveway. I asked the driver to follow James' car as there was no sense in getting out of the taxi when James wasn't going to be home. My taxi followed my husband's car for a distance, and then I watched James park his car, and then both sides of the front doors opened. James got out of the driver's side, and a woman got out of the other. They walked into a restaurant. I paid the taxi driver and went to a café across the road. I supposed that James and the woman were business colleagues, and I didn't want to interrupt a meeting, so I thought I'd wait until they emerged and then surprise James and go home with him.

An hour and a half later, they both emerged. I was about to surprise him when the woman grabbed his hand. I was in total shock; it was so hard to believe. For a moment, I was sure I was wrong, or I thought perhaps James was in a situation where she had grabbed his hand, and he didn't know what to do as he had been caught off guard. Time was standing still for me. I had to pull myself together. I told myself there had to be a reasonable explanation for this. Don't be stupid, calm down, relax, find a taxi and go back to his place, I told myself. It would all be all right. On the taxi ride back, I could hear the sound of my heart thumping. I could almost hear it breaking. I had to stay strong because I wanted to believe I was wrong, mistaken or perhaps a little crazy.

When I finally pulled up in the taxi, James and the woman were walking up to his apartment. He unlocked the door, and they both went inside. I still talked myself into believing they were having a business meeting.

I didn't know what to do. Usually, I would take control, but I could do nothing. I was immobile with shock. Everything seemed to stand still; it was cold, and I was scared. And then the lights went out in his apartment. My familiar, tough exterior broke down. I had nothing, no answers. I got a taxi to take me to the nearest hotel. I kept telling myself a good night's sleep would fix everything, and it would all make more sense in the morning. After many sleepless hours of pacing, staring out the window at nothing and many cups of coffee later, I still couldn't work out what I should do. My head spun with different options. Call him, and if he lies, that will confirm what I was thinking. Call my Mum or sister? I don't know how many times I dialled their numbers. Go back and bang on the door until he answers? For the first time, I wasn't proactive.

I decided to confront him, and so I went back. The sun was now up.

As the taxi pulled up, James and the woman walked down the driveway for what looked like a morning walk. He looked so happy, so free, content even. I was shell-shocked. I wasn't expecting that. I was still halfway out the taxi door when I realised I couldn't handle what I had seen, so I jumped back in and said, "Airport, please."

10. Mea Culpa

I am sure the taxi driver thought I was nuts. James had not seen me. I honestly can't remember what I said or whether I could even speak, but soon, I booked a flight, and the destination was Sydney. It was the worst flight of my life. Stress was not good for my disease, and I was suffering badly. I wasn't supposed to drink, but I was beyond caring. James' smile haunted me all the way home. I would be home by the afternoon. I took two Valiums, closed my eyes and didn't speak to anyone until I had to tell the taxi driver my address. It was hard walking through the door, knowing our lives would never be the same. I felt alone; I was alone, and I needed to be alone. My mobile rang and rang, but I couldn't bring myself to answer it. I had so much to work out.

I had some compulsive traits. Cleaning was one of them. The house had to be clean before I went to Melbourne. I cleaned it again when I got back. I did the washing, ironing, and anything else that needed straightening, fixing, wiping, sweeping, and generally put into place.

I hadn't slept or eaten and had meetings booked on Monday. I had a company to run, and that was what I would do. I thought it would keep me busy and focused. Eating was something I had to do for medical reasons. I was on a strict food regime, and not eating caused many issues. I remember just sitting in the dark, staring at nothing. Then the realisation came to me – he'd looked so happy when I saw him with the other woman. There was something else: my gut reaction was that this affair was not just a physical dalliance. It was an affair of the heart; this devastated me. No affair is acceptable, but I believed that when intense emotions were involved, it was so much more serious. The thought of a purely physical affair was disgusting to me, but I thought that perhaps there would be minimal damage. We could work through it together if we wanted to stay together.

Thoughts of suicide whirled inside my head, but when I thought about leaving my dog, I couldn't do it. I had to think of something else. We had had a very tough year. He was working for me, and we were working in different cities. It was my fault. I'd always told myself I wasn't good enough and had to take the blame and make it easier for him. Perhaps my parents had been right all along. He needed to be happy, and I was holding him back. He needed to start again with someone else. I needed an out. I had to make him hate me. I had to do something unforgivable. I had to give him back his life and make it look like it was all my fault. I was a strong person, so I knew what I had to do would be hard on myself. So, I had to get to work. I didn't tell anyone and couldn't confront James because I felt everything was my fault. I had driven him to this. I couldn't tell my family because they'd immediately blame me.

A major event was coming up and I was working with hundreds of people, so it wasn't that hard to put a plan into action. And I had a plan: pretend to have an affair so that my marriage would fall apart, and James could be free. I had seen how happy he was with the woman in Melbourne. I was convinced she could give him children and bring him what he wanted.

My uncle was working at a development site at the time and knew a man, Brad, who lived near our house. I had an idea and approached them to help me look like I was having an affair by spreading rumours. I let everyone talk, expecting it to get back to my parents. To my surprise, it didn't. My relatives whispered about it to each other and nothing more, so I had to step up the plan. I was self-medicating myself a lot by this stage. Pretending to have an affair is just as stressful as having an affair.

Brad came over one morning as we were going for a drive to be seen together and to discuss how my idea wasn't moving fast enough. As I opened the garage door, my father-in-law was on the other side. In theory, this was perfect, but it was serious. I was not ready for that, and, for a moment, I wanted to end the whole thing. My father-in-law left quickly, not looking back. That was a real low point. I hadn't realised how many others would get hurt until that incident happened. What could I do? I understood what I was doing at that moment. James wasn't the only one; there were so many more people involved that I just hadn't thought about. They would be affected directly and indirectly. I wanted to stop but kept remembering James' face, his smile of contentment. Once again, thoughts of suicide crossed my mind. I couldn't deal with the idea of my father-in-law thinking I was having an affair. I had an agenda, but hurting others was certainly not part of it. I went over to see my in-laws that evening to reassure them that I wasn't having an affair. I didn't tell them I'd planned to make them think I was. I simply told them the truth and that night, it was the truth. I wasn't having an affair. My mother-in- law believed me.

That night was tough. I drove back to our place, just thinking of my options. James deserved a life, one that we knew I couldn't give him. Children were very important to him and not only to him but to me also. I had always imagined having two children and calling them Willow and James, but we discovered it was not meant to be.

Doctors had advised us that my disease could be genetically passed on. James and I digested that information and didn't talk about it. One morning, we were at a shopping centre where people from an organisation were looking for sponsors for children in Africa. I asked James what he thought of my idea; as usual, he left the decision up to me. The child we sponsored was called Moses, and he lived in Africa. If we couldn't have children, then at least we could make a difference in a child's life.

Then something happened that pushed me over the edge; I really did have an affair; my affair with Brad turned real. It had nothing to do with sex. It was the feeling that someone was there for you, thinking about you, striving to be a better person for you. My family had only ever criticised me; James was having an affair, and my future was looking bleak. I simply needed someone to value me.

Friends have asked me why I didn't tell my parents that James was having an affair when I first found out. They suggested that it may have shattered my parents' perception that James was perfect. Perhaps they could see that I was the one wronged. There are reasons why I made the decisions I did. Firstly, my mother would never have believed my husband was having an affair. She would have called me a liar, a bitch, and all the familiar names. Secondly, the idea that I was intrinsically evil was so ingrained in me, and my self-esteem so low that I felt he deserved happiness, and I didn't. I had missed out on my chance of happiness with Christopher, and I had to accept that. I couldn't be the wife James wanted. I was sick, getting progressively worse, and I couldn't have children. Everything that was ingrained in me from my mother came to the fore. Useless. Stupid. Bitch.

Slut. Will never amount to anything. It's all my fault.

I decided that I was not going to stand in James' way. I was going to tell him that I needed some time out. My parents had found out that I did have an affair with Brad, and they called to invite me over for dinner. I needed support and comfort, love and understanding. I thought that perhaps my being totally honest about first pretending to have an affair and then actually really having one and the reasons – because I couldn't make James happy, so I had to break up my marriage – would maybe elicit some sympathy. James was in Sydney and he came with me to my parent's house. My mother lurched into an attack so vicious I was shocked.

She didn't hold back.

"You are nothing but a slut!" she screamed.

She yelled at James, who now knew about my affair. I still didn't tell them that James was the one who started being unfaithful.

"How can you take this bitch back after this?"

My relationship with my mother took a dive. All I had done was try and make things easier for others, but everything was turning out wrongly. I was at a very low point in my life. There didn't seem to be any happiness anywhere.

I can't exactly pinpoint when I started to self-harm. In the beginning, I enjoyed the power and control it gave me. It was my secret; it was something that only I could make decisions about. My mother couldn't make it for me, and she didn't have to know. It was one little victory. I don't know when it changed from power and control to the idea that I deserved to be hurt. Sometimes, while sitting at my desk working, I would bite my fingers where the skin and nails connect. As soon as I felt I had a grasp on the skin, I'd pull it back with my teeth. I'd receive an element of pain or a trickle of blood. I'd stop and go straight to the bathroom and take a first aid kit in with me, where I'd pull off even more skin. Back at my desk, my finger would throb, but I would smile and feel quite impressed with myself.

Over the years, I advanced to punching myself in the face using a blunt object as I believed I deserved it. After many years of seeing a clinical psychologist, I understand I just wanted my internal mental/physical pain/feeling to be seen on the outside. I lost count of the suicide attempts. Despite what many people think – that suicide is the easy way out – it was not an easy decision to consider. I didn't wake up in the morning and tell myself that today was the day I was committing suicide. There was just something inside that didn't want to continue anymore. I felt that I couldn't stand any more being dumped on me. I could see no other way out. There was no way forward; I couldn't go back and undo the past, and life continued, but I didn't want to go forward. No one understood or could see or feel my pain or see the thoughts that ran through my head. It seemed the only option, and there would be no more pain. All gone away. It was September 2002, and I couldn't see myself living past that date.

I called the drug line and made up a story about a friend who had swallowed ten of her brain tablets in the hope that it might kill her. I was wondering whether ten would be enough. The operator confirmed my friend would be fine, very dizzy and would sleep for a couple of days straight. I couldn't ask how many would be needed to kill a person, so I went to bed with a brand-new repeat of two hundred tablets sitting on my chest and a glass of water. I spent the night contemplating whether to take them or not.

That image of James walking down the driveway, smiling and content, was playing inside my head. He deserved to be happy. I was still thinking about how many pills it would take to die when the phone rang. It was my mother. I tried talking to her, but my focus was on the bottle. She could hear something was wrong. I was crying and wasn't making much sense. She thought I was thinking about suicide because of my physical illnesses. She told me to hold on and that she was on her way. I had calmed down and was sitting up in bed by this stage, thinking they would help me. I wasn't going to tell them about James. They already thought I was having an affair. I thought that with everything I had been through already in my short life, an affair that wasn't an affair would be easy. It was terrible; I never realised how disgusted I was with myself. The thought of having an affair was appalling, but not having one and saying you are having one and then really having one made me feel dreadful.

I knew deep down that one of the reasons James was seeing another woman was because his dream of having children would never come true if he stayed with me. Perhaps it didn't enter his head that there are other ways of making a family; adoption and surrogacy obviously weren't good enough.

I also had to acknowledge that he didn't want a career woman. He wanted a stay-at-home wife. It was the reverse situation that he'd grown up with. James' father had stayed at home. He did the paperwork for the family business and domestic duties. James' mother was the driven one, the one with business acumen. James wanted a wife who was going to stay home with the children. He didn't have the guts to say so, but I knew that's what he wanted. He wanted to be the alpha breadwinner and would have never been a stay-at-home Dad. I would have taken a step back. I would have been like most modern mothers who stay home for some time and then resume their careers. He was happy at the beginning that I was a successful businesswoman. We never discussed what would happen when we had children, but I know he would have expected me to give up my career. That wasn't me. I was happy training people, firing people, kicking ass all the way to the top. He didn't understand or didn't want to believe that women could have a family and a career.

Much later, I heard about some statistics that relate to what happens when one partner is diagnosed with a serious disease like mine or multiple sclerosis. In many cases, where the man is diagnosed with a serious illness, the woman stays and cares for him. When the situation is reversed, many men leave.

My sister and niece arrived, as my mother told them something was wrong. My sister took the bottle of tablets away from me just as my parents arrived. My father was compassionate and sat beside me. He told me that I hadn't committed a crime, hadn't killed anyone, and therefore, I was to stop giving myself such a hard time. My father then went out of the room to make a phone call. My mother started as soon as my father was out of the room. She was ropable; angry because I wanted to speak to my father first and not to her.

"So, you ring and speak to your father first rather than your own mother!"

I didn't understand her anger. I would have thought that her priority would be to see if I was all right, not to go on about who I spoke to first.

My sister Tegan came into the room and told me that my Dad had just called Brett and told him he was going to kill him and never to contact me again. I quickly took the rest of the tablets. Tegan saw me do it and screamed out to Mum. Mum came running in and then screamed at me.

"I didn't almost die giving birth to you so that you can commit suicide now!" she screamed.

She pulled me out of bed, threw me on the floor and pulled me back up. She pushed me out of the house and kicked me all the way to the car. When I tried to pull away, she kicked me hard in the back of the knees. I lay down in the back of the car, my legs throbbing in pain. I felt the car reversing, and then I blacked out. I awoke to a bright light shining in my eyes. A man was holding a torch over my face. I told him to go away and that I just wanted to sleep. Other people held me down while the man examined my eyes. He told my mother to take me home and let me sleep it off and that I needed to be taken to a hospital in another two days. I didn't understand any of this.

"After everything I've done for her, this is how she repays me!" my mother cried. "How selfish! Can't she see how much I'm suffering?"

Two days later, I heard my mother on the phone trying to get me committed to Callan Park psychiatric hospital. I had recovered from the overdose but was still groggy and didn't quite understand what was going on around me. My mother came into the bedroom and spoke to me. She hadn't managed to get me scheduled, but she had Plan B in action. Her tone of voice was angry.

"You need time out and rest, and you are going to St. John of God hospital." She told me all about the hospital, making it sound like a luxury retreat with spas and pampering facilities. I didn't argue with her. I desperately wanted James to stand up for me and be supportive when my mother criticised me, but I didn't and couldn't stand up for myself, and in some ways, I was unfair pointing the finger at him when I couldn't do what I wanted him to do. She was Mum and she knew best. I sat thinking about the man I had given up. I'd lost him forever. For what?

I worked out pretty quickly what sort of place it was. I had a private room on the ground floor, which I suspected was for people like me. The second floor was reserved for more severe cases. It was lunchtime when I arrived. I was given medication. Mum said she would come and have lunch with me every day. She never came back for lunch. Ever.

Later, I found out that after my mother had kicked me so viciously, she had a fear that she was turning into her violent father, and she didn't want to follow in his footsteps. She made an appointment with a psychiatrist to discuss the issue. She went once and never returned. She didn't like the psychiatrist. She made an appointment with another psychiatrist and then another. She made more appointments. She went to each of them once, six in total. She didn't like any of them. I believe she didn't like them because she didn't want to hear the truth about herself. My father was no better in his understanding of his wife needing help.

"Look what you've done to your mother! You've driven her so crazy that she has to see a shrink!"

Once again, it was *my* fault that my mother wasn't coping with whatever that incident had brought up. I was so doped up when I first arrived at the hospital I didn't realise that the place I was in wasn't a health spa. I wondered why nurses would be needed at a spa.

Medicating myself was difficult as medication was in the nurses' hands. We had to line up to get our drugs. A few patients had worked out how to get what they needed, and they taught me how to do it. I became dependent on numbing my pain. I had to be careful and use my medication sparingly as I never knew when I'd be able to get more. I wasn't allowed to go anywhere for the first twenty-four hours. I wondered whether there was a gym. I found a chapel instead. The backs of my legs and knees sported blue-black bruises where my mother had kicked me. They were sore for a week.

Attending group sessions, I realised that many people were just like me. Many of the sessions dealt with feelings and actions that related directly to me. I wasn't the only one who cut herself or the only one who had had many suicide attempts. Other people were feeling as lonely, depressed, rejected, and disappointed with life as I was. Sometimes, when particular topics came up, I felt like they referred specifically to me. It was comforting to understand that others had histories of self-harm, aching loneliness, wrecked marriages, different addictions, low self-esteem, had endured various forms of abuse and had self-medicated in ways that let out the pain. Sometimes, I would look around the room and think, 'I'm nothing like these people,' but as time passed, I realised that I was very much like them, and they were like me. Many had dysfunctional mothers as well.

There were moments of laughter amidst all the pain of being in a psychiatric hospital. One morning, one of the patients was crying. I asked her why she was upset; she said it was her birthday.

"And look where I am," she said.

"Well, it's not the best health spa," I said, "but it could be worse."

The other patients began to laugh, and so did the woman who had been crying.

"Melissa, you're not at a health spa; you're in St John of God," they all said. By this time, I was having fun.

"Really? What a weird name for a health spa."

When everyone finally realised I was having a joke, they all started laughing with me, and the best thing about it was that the woman who had been crying was now laughing as well.

My mother visited with James soon after I was admitted. Her first question was not about how I was doing. She was like a hawk, poised over my bed, demanding answers to her questions.

"Do many people know about this affair? Who have you told?"

She then told me that if any of my siblings' or friends' marriages were to fail in the future, it would be my fault. James said nothing. I was a bad influence on everyone, a terrible role model for younger people, my mother told me. James still said nothing. We cried, hugged each other, and held hands.

James, his Dad, and his brother came to visit. Only my mum, dad and James came into my room that day. His Dad and brother stayed outside the room. My mother started yelling at me about the affair. She called me a slut, a bitch, a whore. I couldn't stand it anymore and shouted out for the nurse. I asked them to remove my mother.

The staff removed everyone.

A friend came to the hospital to visit me. He told me later about his exchange with my mother when he came out of my room after seeing me. My mother was sitting on a chair in the waiting room and saw my friend coming out of my room.

"So, she's fucking you now, is she?"

"*Excuse me?*"

"You just came out of Melissa's room, didn't you?" My friend said that he had.

"So, she's fucking you now, is she? You're the flavour of the month for that slut, are you?" My friend was shocked.

"Melissa is a good friend and a lovely person, and she's going through a really bad patch at the moment," my friend fired back.

"Oh, then you don't really know her at all," my mother replied. "You have no idea of what's she like."

My friend turned away from my mother and walked out the door.

While I was recovering in the hospital, my mother decided that my marriage was over. She told me that she had spoken to James, and the upshot was that we would get a divorce and that I would move back home and live with her and my father. I was too ill to fight back. It was a forgone conclusion. Mum knew best. Just as I'd had no say in my marriage and wedding day, I now had no say in its demise. I would never be with the man I loved or get to marry him. It was all too late. Mum had told James that I had had another affair. This was a lie because I had only one affair, the one with Brad, which I had confessed to, and I couldn't comprehend why she would tell James this. I had to explain to him that this new piece of information wasn't the truth, and all I could do was hope that he believed me rather than my mother. I knew that I had to take back control of my own life, thinking it was easy, but I was still too sick to take control. I heard a song one morning, Vanessa Amorosi's *The Power*. That song spoke to me. It's the power I want. It's the power I need.

> *Unlike a miracle or a wish upon a star*
> *The power to be me is all I need to start*
> *To do things I'll never regret*
> *And to leave the rest behind*

I had that song on replay. I listened to it constantly. It kept me going in my darkest moments. When I thought there was no hope and I wouldn't ever have the strength to get better and decide what I was going to do, I'd put on that song. It was my mantra. There were times when it literally saved me from trying to end my life again. That song will always have a special place in my heart.

My sister-in-law came into my hospital room one morning. She wasn't there to see how I was doing. She was there to deliver the news that I was now on the outer.

"We never wanted you as a godmother to our child. We only wanted James as godfather."

She'd told me this before the christening, and now I was hearing it again. My two sisters and a long-time family friend were next to come in.

They, too, had not come to see how I was but to criticise. As sick as I was, I knew that everyone had fallen for the perception of me that my mother had given them. Her lies had brainwashed them.

That morning, some sliver of doubt came up from somewhere inside me. Was my mother always right? Was it possible that she could be wrong? For the first time, I wondered about her; I really wondered why she did this. For the first time, I began to question whether she did know what was best for me. Why did she seem to hate me so much when all I did was try to please her? I didn't understand. Added to this, I had always really believed on some level that everything was my fault. I didn't know how to form any other opinion; I was used to being the hopeless one who always disappointed everyone and excelled at my job. I was confused.

I lay back on my pillows, exhausted. I had a life-threatening illness, a disintegrating marriage, an unfaithful husband, a business I was too ill to run, a mother who blamed me for everything, a suicide attempt, and a future of total uncertainty. Also, I found out that Brad had told my Dad he had fallen in love with me.

It made me utterly miserable.

Towards the end of my stay at St John of God, I was doing a jigsaw puzzle when people began to file into the room. I was asked if I wanted to participate in an activity, and I declined, continuing to focus on my puzzle. I assumed it was some sort of religious class as a nun and priest were carrying pictures. The group started to organise the room for their activity. They sat in a circle. The nun placed a heap of images on the carpet and told everyone to take two. One image, she told the group, represented our past and the other, our future. I was intrigued, so I turned around and was drawn to the images on the floor. I decided to join in, and I chose two pictures. We then each had a turn explaining to the rest of the group why we had chosen these particular images.

The first picture I chose was of a finger held over a chess piece on a chessboard. The way the finger was hovering resonated with me. It was all about the next move. For me, the next move had always been made. I was the chess piece being moved around with no say in my life. It was such a simple image, but it struck a chord deep inside me. The movers were other people who thought they knew what was best for me. The tough decisions I made at work and the responsibility that they carried were never acknowledged by my family. My career was the only place where I made the decisions. The chess piece didn't know which way the hand would move it; it was unsure of what the next move would be. The hand had the power. That power was the power of my family. Every decision had been orchestrated by my mother.

The second picture I chose was of hands cupped together. Inside the hands was a tiny tree growing up between the hands. That tree was me, struggling to grow, find a place, have my voice heard, and carve out a future where I could grow and flourish. That tree was beautiful. I had always been told I was useless and had been put down by my mother and sisters. My self-esteem had always been low, but I could be like the tree. I could have a future.

Two very simple pictures held much meaning for me. I sat there and explained to a group of strangers about how my mother had always treated me. As I spoke, others nodded and encouraged me to talk. I spoke about the images' meaning for me, and as I did so, a vast wave of release swept over me. I felt the empathy of others. I felt the power of those images. It moved me emotionally and mentally. The others could see what an impact this exercise had on me. The other patients commented on my analysis. Thought-provoking and brilliant were some of the comments I received. Some others also spoke about terrible family relationships, so I didn't feel so alone.

Nobody came the day I was discharged. Not one member of my family. My car was parked at the hospital, and I drove to my parents' house. I needed to retrieve some of my belongings. I went down the side of the house to enter it as I didn't want to run into my mother. After collecting everything I needed, I ran into Dad. He told me James was continually whining about money and didn't have enough to live on. My father asked me to take some money from the business to give to James. I explained that I just couldn't take money out of the business, that it didn't work like that. My father didn't understand anything about personal and business finances being separate and the fact that I had to account for why money would be taken out of the business and for what purpose. It would muck up things with taxation as well. In the end, I had to take money out of the business. I gave it to my father and told him to give it to James. Then I told him I didn't ever want to hear about James having no money ever again.

When I got to the house James and I had bought, my family was there to help start moving everything out. There had been no discussion with me about this; it was just accepted that the marriage was over and that I would no longer live in the house. James was there, crying, walking around in circles. I watched as my family went around the house, touching all my things, picking them up, wrapping and packing stuff for James. At times, when they'd pick up a particular object, I would start to cry. Their response was always the same.

"Well, it's all your fault."

"You brought this on yourself."

"James deserves someone better," my mother said as she wrapped a vase in newspaper.

While the others were packing up my stuff, James and I walked around the house, holding hands. We sat down on the floor and cried. We talked about my affair, the real one I had. James said he could never trust me again. We talked about counselling, but nothing was correctly sorted. He kept telling me I should try rebuilding my relationship with my family. I couldn't understand how he could say this when he knew the cruelty they had meted out while I was in St John of God hospital. One of the things that was bothering me was also the fact that I was having trouble with my guilt over my affair, and that led me to a question: Did James feel any guilt over *his* affair? Did he honestly think I didn't know? How could he be judgemental towards me for my indiscretion, yet he had done the same? How could he be so self-righteous about trust and betrayal? I didn't tell him about the fake affair or discuss the reason for the real affair. I was still convinced he deserved happiness with someone and with a woman who could give him children.

At one point, I was on the verge of discussing everything with him, finally getting it all out with no secrets between us. I was about to talk about going to counselling, but we were suddenly interrupted. My mother entered the room where James and I were sitting on the floor.

"What are you doing holding hands with that bitch?" she asked him. "Don't even think of taking her back."

I waited for James to tell my mother not to call me a bitch. I waited for him to tell her I had had a tough time and needed support, not criticism. I knew then that if our marriage had any chance of surviving, we would have to leave the country or move interstate, and that just wasn't possible. My mother was trying to sabotage my attempts to reconcile with James and save my marriage.

I waited for him to tell her to leave the room and let us talk. He did nothing. I knew then that James and I were truly over. He couldn't stand up for me or even for himself. He had never stood up for me in front of my mother. Never.

"You've never stood up for me."

He remained silent. He'd once told me that I'd made him look weak. Now I realised he *was* weak. He let go of my hand. My mother smiled. She looked at James, and I could read the look in her eyes. It almost looked like lust for him. My sister told me on the same day that the family wanted to have an intervention to 'help' me. I told her no. I knew then that any intervention from them would not be helpful; it would merely be another platform for them to drag me down even further, spearheaded by my mother.

My mother hurled another grenade in my direction later that day.

"If you come over to visit our house and James is there, then you have to leave."

I was obviously a terrible person. My mother seemed obsessed with keeping James and me apart. They didn't even want me in the same room as my estranged husband. I couldn't understand why I was so tainted. Many people had done far worse things than I ever had, but it seemed I was lumped in with the worst. Many people have affairs, but the way my mother was going on about it put it in the same class as murder or child trafficking.

I made myself a promise the day I collected my belongings from my parent's home, the home where I grew up. It was all too painful, too complicated, too confusing. I didn't know whose fault anything was anymore. I only knew one thing: I would never step foot in that house ever again.

11. Hurt Me

Miranda was my new home. I had a small three-bedroom townhouse. All my furniture was in storage. I was starting my life all over again.

I kept to my routine and started going to church at Northbridge. I was doing even management and organising fashion parades at major shopping centres. I worked every day, including weekends. While I was in St John of God, I wrote goodbye notes: one to my husband and one to my mother and father. I was feeling so bad about the affair, feeling that I had shamed my mother, father and husband. I didn't deserve to have them in my life. My mother was right about me.

While I was unpacking my stuff that wasn't in storage, I became upset that three pieces of Swarovski crystal that James had given me were missing. He had given them to me as presents on three separate occasions, and even though we were no longer together, they had great sentimental value for me. They were a bell, a rose, and a bear. I asked my sister if she knew what had happened to the crystal.

"I haven't got them. Are you saying one of us took them?"

"No, I am not. I am just asking as I am sure someone took them to keep them safe."

I was cautious with my words. I wanted to ask who had taken or even stolen them, but I knew I wouldn't get an answer if I said that. I never saw the crystal again. I was upset about the missing pieces. Andrew took a few things that day and said he was taking them for James. This did not sit well with me, but I accepted it. I felt like taking legal action to get the pieces back, as they meant so much to me, but I didn't have the energy to do anything about it.

I wanted nothing from my family, but I still felt a connection with my father, and sometimes I'd ring to speak to him. If my mother answered the phone, she'd quietly say to me, "Oh, the slut is on the phone," and then she'd yell out to my Dad, "Melissa's on the phone."

Over time, her words seeped into my head. Slut. I was a slut. That's what I came to believe. My self-esteem plummeted. I was a terrible person. I wasn't fit to be around my nieces and nephews as I was an immoral influence. I was not a good role model. While in hospital, I felt supported. I had psychologists on hand and others around me who had been in black places and understood. Now that I didn't have that support around me, I slipped back quickly into what was familiar – that I was a bad person. With no support, the negative thoughts started whirling, the self-harm started up, and ideas about ending it all rose to the surface. The thoughts went round and round in my head. Slut. Stupid. Useless. Bad influence. Failure. Good for nothing. You deserve it.

My father wasn't always helpful. One night, not long after I'd moved into my new place, I found myself thinking about suicide. I felt I just couldn't go on. I was highly emotional and needed someone to speak to. It was the 17 November 2002.

"Dad, I'm not doing so well," I said. "I'm thinking about killing myself." There was a slight pause before my father spoke.

"Melissa, it's late, and I have to get up early in the morning. Can you call one of your friends?"

That conversation with my father tipped me over the edge. I took an overdose that night and ended up in Sutherland Hospital. The doctors pumped out my stomach; I rested for a while and was discharged. The staff weren't convinced I wouldn't try suicide again, but they let me leave with no follow-up. It was a strange situation. On one hand, preserve my life with the drugs I had to take and on the other, contemplating suicide with other drugs. It depended on what was happening that day or night. It was like a seesaw. During the days, I'd take my drugs to combat the symptoms of the disease, but on many nights, I'd add up how many other drugs I'd need to end it all. Up, down. Up, down. Live. Die. Live. Die. Good day. Bad night. Bad day. Good night. Pills that kept me alive. Pills that could see me dead. Even though my Dad didn't seem to be able to understand my pain and didn't have any empathetic resources, I still felt closer to him than the rest of the family.

I rang him one afternoon while still living in Miranda. I then asked if I could speak to my mother.

"Hi, Mum," I said. "I've missed you and love you."

When those words came tumbling out, I realised then that I still wanted her love and approval. I hadn't entirely written off a relationship with her even though I wasn't deserving of her love. Despite her cruelty towards me, there was still the tug of mother love-approval going on inside me.

"You're a slut," she said. "You waste money," she said.

"You didn't deserve James," she said. "You're a piece of dirt." I started to cry. She listened to me sobbing over the phone. "I hate you," she said, then hung up.

I was devastated. Why did she hate me so much? I tried one more time. I rang at night, and my mother answered the phone.

"Hi Mum, it's me. I just called to tell you I love you."

"You disgust me, and I am ashamed of you. James deserved someone better than you. You are a slut, worthless, and I have no time for you. You have hurt so many people, including me, your sisters, your brother, James, and his family. All you really think about is yourself. You are good for nothing. I always said you walked around with a sign on your head, 'Asking for It'."

Asking for it?

Asking for what? Asking for a brutal disease that was ruining my life? I was so shocked I started to cry. My mother had no sympathy.

"No, no, don't start crying. I can't look at you or even talk to you."

I couldn't stand to hear another word. I told my mother as calmly as possible that I was sorry for calling and wasn't rude, but I had to go. I broke down completely as soon as I replaced the phone on the hook. I wanted to take an overdose but didn't have any medication in the house. I had no answers as to why my mother hated me so much. Surely, I couldn't be that bad?

I knew that I couldn't have a relationship with my mother anymore. I was cutting her out. It was easy to say this. It was more difficult to accept that this was what I had to do. All I ever wanted was her love. All she ever gave me was criticism. It would be many years before I understood why she was so cruel.

I would often get phone calls from my father regarding the settlement. He seemed to be intervening on behalf of James. In the end, James got far more than was fair, but I was so battered by the continual demands and interference that I gave in. At times, my father would yell at me over the phone. It seemed very strange that my family would go into bat for their son-in-law for more than what was fair. Why wouldn't they want the best for their daughter? My father's attitude to my doing so well in my career path was also not encouraging. Despite being so ill and having stints in hospital, large companies still head-hunted me. I had accepted work for a huge corporation and was immensely proud of the work I was doing. I told my father all about it.

"That's what James does," he said. "That's what *I* do," I said.

"But you're a girl," he said.

"Yes, a girl who has a much higher position than James, a girl who was his boss and a girl who earns much more than James as well."

They were prouder of James than their own daughter. My father just didn't get it. But you're a girl. What was that supposed to mean? That it couldn't be true because of my gender? Did he think I was making it up? Did he not believe that women can earn higher salaries than men? Did he think that James was the highflyer and I was his assistant? As frustrated as I felt, there was nothing I could say that was going to change his attitude. Decades of male-dominated culture were too hard to break. That macho Maltese upbringing and his father's attitudes had been deeply driven into his thinking. It wouldn't have mattered if I was a CEO, earning millions; there was a part of him that was in denial about what women could achieve.

Despite the progress that I made, major depression plagued me, and in November 2002, I took an overdose and ended up in hospital. My parents came to visit, but I didn't want my mother in the room. My father came in to see me, and although I was pleased to see him, I knew he didn't understand about depression and what it can do.

"OK. Don't you think it's time to move on?" he asked. "It's time to grow up; it's time to stop being silly."

My father could not either understand or accept that depression was anything other than being 'silly' or due to some state of immaturity.

I had managed to smuggle boxes of Panadol into my room, and I went into the toilet and tried to swallow the lot. A young nurse who was very aware of what some patients like me often do wasn't going to let me get away with anything. She told another nurse that I had been in the toilet too long, and so they burst in and caught me trying to take the pills. I hadn't swallowed many. The nurses seem annoyed.

"We're here to help you so you can leave hospital, but by doing this, you're making it more difficult to leave."

"We're transferring you to a psych ward," they told me.

There was no bed available in the psychiatric ward, so I was moved to a general ward where I had to share a room with three other people. I spent two nights there before being transferred to a psychiatric ward. I was finally discharged a few days later. I went back to work as though nothing had happened. It was the only way to survive.

Christmas 2002 had come and gone. James and I saw each other a few times after I moved to Miranda, but it was just too difficult. I had bought him a Christmas present, so I thought I'd drop it off at his parents' place. As pulled into the driveway, a strange sense of eeriness washed over me. Here I was delivering his Christmas present, and we were separated, divorce pending. I was also dropping off the dog as I couldn't take care of him due to it being New Year's Eve. I had a big night ahead of me as I was second in command of the New Year's Eve event in the Royal Botanic Gardens. A night of heavy responsibility would be in full swing in a couple of hours, and I needed to be on the ball at all times. I noticed a car I'd never seen before in the driveway of James parents' home, a four-wheel drive. James' Mum came out to greet me, and I soon forgot about the mystery car. I told her that I'd put the present for James in his room. His mother went to get dressed for work. I crept into James room. The curtains were drawn, so it was quite dark in the room. I put the present on his desk. I bent over to kiss him, trying not to wake him. He turned in his sleep, and I quickly backed out of the room. He didn't wake. I yelled goodbye to his parents and drove away.

Not long after that, I was driving when my mobile rang. "Mum said you just called in. Why didn't you wake me?"

I told him that I'd crept into his room but didn't want to wake him. "That wasn't me. I was sleeping in my brother's room."

"Then who was in your room?"

"That was Tanya. She's staying over coz we're going away for a few days."

Tanya was the woman who James had worked with at the first centre.

I had to concentrate on the road, so I breathed deeply until I got to work. I had a huge day and night ahead and had to be up for the job. I felt sick. I'd been replaced and not only had I been replaced; I'd almost kissed the new girlfriend.

I don't know how I got through that day and the night, but I did, throwing myself into work, doing my job as well as I could. That night I did my job one hundred and ten per cent, and at the same time, I was crumbling inside.

I was working on a contract with the Botanical Gardens in Sydney. I knew my body was changing, and some parts weren't working like they used to, but I went into denial and worked even harder. It was January 2003. At that time, I often didn't sleep for up to four days at a time and lived on coffee and adrenalin. I was on edge the whole time because of the responsibility. I wasn't dealing with my illness. Instead, I was pushing it down, pretending it wasn't there.

"Go away," I said to Cerebral Atrophy. "I'm not taking notice of you at the moment. I'm far too busy. I've got things to do."

I was just beginning to make my way in events management and didn't want to think that there would come a time when I couldn't do it anymore. Although it could be stressful, I was very excited about the contracts I was getting. I worked for the Big Day Out and worked on the tour for the singer Anastacia. Anastacia was lovely, but the work was gruelling. One of the longest days I did was while working on that tour. There was an afternoon where Anastacia did signings for fans when they bought the album. The queue was very long. Singers get royalties from every sale, but I got the impression that Anastacia wasn't doing it for that reason. She enjoyed meeting her fans. I waited for her people to tell me to cut the queue off, but they didn't. She signed for hours while I sat on the big black equipment boxes and waited. I was exhausted when I got home. I knew I was overworking, but it was my way of soothing the anxiety and creating a buffer between myself and the harsh aspects of reality and the even harsher ones that deep down I knew the future would bring.

Once again, I worked Tropfest and put in long hours.

I was on my own, trying to make a life, juggling my health and a career, and trying to get over the past events and the hurt that my family had inflicted on me.

I had reached a new all-time low. I couldn't stay at my residence anymore.

The new year came. January 2003. I had finished the contract with the Royal Botanic Gardens. I went back to consulting and changed my company name. By that time, I was living at Cronulla with my friend, Cam, in an apartment. By February I had contracts all over Sydney. I worked for Tropfest in March 2003. I was the assistant production manager and site manager. I went to Kuala

Lumpur for a holiday. The X Games were on, and I was working on management for some events.

The Easter Show was about to start, and I had long hours and double shifts. I threw myself into work and still had to keep doctors' appointments and try to look after my health as best I could. It was difficult, but I managed to do my job. My eyesight had begun to fail, and I was having trouble reading. I still had the tremors in my arms and legs and terrible headaches.

"Please don't take my eyesight. I need it for work. It'll kill me. Just don't. I can handle the headaches. Give me more of those but not eyesight."

"Don't bargain with me," said Cerebral Atrophy. "I do what I want when I want."

In June 2003, I tried my hand at television. I put my name down at an agency and got quite a bit of work, mainly as an extra and primarily for alcoholic drinks; quite ironic as I didn't drink. A lot of adds were for overseas television. It was tiring work as whenever the main actor made a mistake there would be re-take. Sometimes this went on for hours. I spent some time with friends, but inside I was missing James and missing my old life. Even though he had mistreated me, I still clung to the memories.

My Dad was starting to ring me and passing on complaints from James about money.

The divorce and property settlement with James went back and forth. In August I had a massive fight with my father over this. Dad wanted me to accept a figure that just wasn't fair. My lawyers didn't think it was fair either. Dad was angry with me. James was whinging, and Dad was sick of it. He just wanted everything finalised. I knew that my mother was behind all the pressure to give James money. He would have been complaining to her, and she would have pressured my father to deal with it.

I explained to my father that my lawyers had said that the sum that my father suggested was a joke. James was certainly not entitled to the amount that my father was suggesting. He still didn't understand. I could not get my head around the fact that my Dad seemed to care more about the amount that James was to get rather than see that his own daughter, who had a brain disease, was looking at an uncertain future and would need finances, settled and secure. Added to that, I had worked extremely hard to get where I was, and James was not entitled to the amounts that he thought he was entitled to. I had made that money in my own right, and it wasn't fair that someone who I was no longer with was making demands on it. Didn't James realise that he still had decades left in his career? He had the chance to make money for a long time into the future, not to mention superannuation. Didn't he understand that a brain disease didn't just go away? Was it so difficult to understand that my disease would cut my career short and that my future was uncertain?

I ploughed on through, throwing myself into my job. Part of the way I got through was being able to tackle things at work in an assertive manner. Delegating and organising were skills at which I was excellent. I knew I was putting up walls emotionally, but it was my way of surviving. I didn't have the physical or emotional energy to engage with anyone other than on a purely professional basis. To understand that your body is breaking down is one thing. Intellectually, I understood what was happening, but when those physical signs happen, despite all the preparation, it's devastating. My ritual had changed. I wasn't the one doing the talking.

"I'm here now," said Cerebral Atrophy. "I'm not going away. You're going to have to deal with me."

Headaches were now a daily occurrence, nausea, and balance issues as well. I was imploding, but no one would know. The walls were going up. I put on my mask.

—

I was sitting on the Esplanade at Manly one evening, thinking about stopping the divorce and trying counselling again. It was January 2004. I rang James, but he was distant. He told me it was too late. Just sign all the papers and let's get on with this, he told me. I sat, watching the sunset, immobilised.

The next afternoon my friend, Cam, took control. I told her what happened over the last few days. She wanted me to feel better.

"Right, Melissa," she said. "Put on something that makes you feel good, do your hair, fix your face, we're going out. I need alcohol, and yes, you will have water. You need to get out for the day and not sit here feeling like you're feeling." Cam was in the same business as I was, but that day she only had two centres to visit and report on. We went to one of the centres she worked on, and I had water. At the next centre, Cam went off to complete her job, and I had time to myself. This was the centre where James worked and I knew he'd be there somewhere. I called centre management and told them that my name was Gail, and I wanted to see James. I knew that if I'd said the name Melissa, then he wouldn't come. A few minutes later, James walked through to where we were to meet. As soon as he saw me, the smile vanished from his face.

James suggested that we go up to the rooftop to talk. I followed him up the stairs. We discussed things amicably for a while. I told him I was moving on with my life. I just wanted to make sure we were on the same page about the divorce, I told him.

"You're not here to discuss the divorce stuff," he said. "You're here about the baby thing, aren't you?"

Irritation rose inside me.

"I'm not cut up about not having a baby with you. Don't be stupid, you know I can't have children."

"Not your baby. My baby. We've had a baby. I'm a father."

He delivered this information as though he was checking off a shopping list. I said nothing for a while, barely believing what I'd just heard. It was the ultimate insult. And there was more to come. Tears were forming.

"You know all that baby stuff that we bought together when we thought we could have kids, the stroller, bassinet and all that linen and clothes? Well, baby stuff is expensive, so could we have all of that stuff? I mean, you'll never use them, there are six plastic storage tubs of the stuff. Shouldn't let it go to waste."

I held his gaze and then spoke in a calm and determined manner.

"There is no way that you are getting any of the baby stuff. That stuff was meant for us, not for you and her. Forget it. Buy your own bloody baby clothes." His manner was strange. He wasn't exactly shouting his happiness at fatherhood from the rooftops. He talked in a very matter-of-fact manner. His tone was flat. I had a hunch that his new girlfriend had snared him by becoming pregnant. We went back and forth for a while, circling over the same old stuff. He said that I had put the dog before him in our relationship. What a joke. He had put my mother before me in our relationship. I left him on the rooftop and went back downstairs.

The amount of emotional pain I was in that day is something that no words can describe adequately. It would have been better if we hadn't met and had just worked things out through solicitors. He knew I could not have children, and the disease would progress. He knew my dream of starting a family had been shattered. How could he be so cruel? Was he so lacking in emotional intelligence that he wouldn't think that a conversation like that was appropriate with me? What the hell was he thinking? Did it not cross his mind that everything that I had lost was now thrown in my face?

It was a mistake to see him again. I was shaking. I needed to be numb. I wanted to bleed out my pain, to feel it on my skin. I was howling loudly, so much, so that staff and customers were coming out of their shops to see what was happening. I felt like a freak.

"Where's the nearest tattoo parlour?" I asked my friend. So, caught up in his own life and the cost of fatherhood that he couldn't even stop to think of what impact his news and the way he imparted it would have on me. People often make thoughtless and hurtful comments to those who can't or don't have children. Often it isn't intentional. I sat through my tattoo procedure, wanting it to hurt much more. It wasn't enough. I chose a star because that was a reminder of my grandmother. I wanted the tattooist to ram that needle in harder. Make me bleed.

More. More.

Hurt me. Hurt me.

Cam didn't cope with the pain of the tattooing very well. She grimaced and looked pale. Years of self-harm had given me a very high pain threshold, and I chatted and laughed with the tattooist while Cam stated that she couldn't believe I wasn't feeling the same level of pain that she was. She couldn't drive home as her pain was too great, so I did the driving.

My health was slowly deteriorating. I went back to having infusions with an environmental doctor. I was supposed to have six but only ended up having one and a half as I couldn't cope with the pain. The infusions caused an intense burning sensation, and I couldn't manage. The infusions had bleach in them, causing my whole body to feel like it was on fire. Apparently, this was a trend at the time. I don't know if it's even legal. I've googled it and can't find any doctors that do this procedure.

Relations with my family were now very strained, but I thought I could at least maintain contact with my siblings. I dropped around to see Amanda one night and things seemed to be all right between us until she started talking about how I had had sex with someone besides James in the house I shared with him. I told her that it was true that I'd had sex with Brad and it happened in the marital bed. Neither statement was true.

I was shocked and annoyed that she would casually mention this. She then told me that she had been talking to James three days ago.

"What? You're in contact with James?"

"Of course. He's my brother-in-law."

I told her that he was her *ex*-brother-in-law.

"Anyway," she said, "he is the trustee of my estate and the godfather of Andrew's daughter, so he will always be part of the family."

I was utterly stunned. *Trustee*? *Godfather*? My ex-husband still in *their* lives? Not only were they emotionally tying themselves with James; now, it was legally binding as well. I was informed that the rest of the family kept in contact with James and had dinner regularly with him. My family was twisting the knife. I was so hurt. I ended up screaming at Amanda and walking out. I decided to go back to my family home and say goodbye. I had to end it properly. When I entered the kitchen, my niece was sitting there.

"Who are you again?" she asked.

I turned to my niece and said, "I am no one."

I walked out of the kitchen and passed my father on the way out. "See you soon," my father said.

Anger boiled inside me.

"No, you won't. I'm never coming back here ever again. This is the last time you'll see me."

My father followed me to my car. He asked what was wrong. My mother came out as well.

"You have to ask? Really?" My voice was rising.

"Can we take this inside, please. We don't want the neighbours hearing everything."

I told him I wasn't going back inside.

"My life is hard enough, what with all the medical stuff. I'm sick and tired of having to work so hard to please you. Everyone in this family is so judgemental.

Mum's been calling me a slut for two years. Yes, that's right, you have," I said to my mother, who was now standing behind him.

My father looked shocked.

"Your mother wouldn't speak like that," my father said.

"Oh, come on, you know she calls me that. And she said if James comes over, then I have to leave.'

My father stated that my mother would never have said that.

"Well, gee, Dad, you'd better check with your wife because that's what she said."

"James is a better person than you," my mother said.

I opened the door to my car. My father tried to stop me. "Melissa, don't drive. You're not well. You shouldn't be driving." I turned and faced both.

"Please don't start showing concern for my failing health now. You know how sick I am, but you still didn't support me. You show love to James but not to me. I'm not jumping through Mum's stupid and mean hoops anymore. Goodbye, Dad, I will never call or visit or be a part of this thing you call 'a family' ever again."

My father put out his hand to stop me, but I pushed past him and got into my car. I drove away and I knew, I was determined, it would be the last time I would see my mother ever again.

It was time to say goodbye.

12. **The Karen Cult**

I finished at the Botanical Gardens in February and did a bit of consulting work for people that I knew. I did Tropfest again in March and also did some work in television advertisements. Some consulting work came up in some Shopping centres, and so I took on a bit of that as well. In April, I was busy with event work at the Royal Easter Show and a bit of consulting, but I was not doing well physically or mentally. The finalisation of the divorce was looming, and I was despondent. I was becoming very uncoordinated as well and very tired, but I pushed myself to keep going.

I had recently undergone some scans as the neurologist was concerned about my growing symptoms. I had a follow-up appointment booked in two weeks. One morning the neurologist rang me and asked me to come in. He told me he needed to see me earlier. While I was speaking to him, I sensed that it was bad news. I was listening to him while not realising that I was talking to my disease at the same time.

"So, you wouldn't stay in your box, CA? Typical!"

"Excuse me?" said the neurologist.

"Sorry," I said. "I can come in at eight in the morning." My neurologist told me he'd see me then.

The next morning, I sat in his office, feeling anxious. He asked me if I wanted James and my mother to come in as well. He thought they were waiting outside. "No, it's just me from now on," I said. "No mother and no husband. Things have changed. So, what's the good news?"

I laughed at that point as I knew it wasn't going to be good. Laughing was the only way I was going to get through the next few minutes.

The neurologist sat forward.

"Your MRI scans show the disease has moved into both sides of your cerebellum."

I sat for a few seconds.

"OK. So am I going to die?"

"Unfortunately, the scans show that it is progressing. I'm very sorry." I nodded.

"Anything else?" I asked.

"We need to increase your medication."

We spoke for a while about medication and therapy, and then I took my prescription and left his office. When I got into the elevator, I pressed G for ground. I didn't feel the sensation of the elevator dropping floors. Time was standing still. This wasn't real. Nothing was real. The doors opened, and I stepped outside.

"All right, I'm going to die," I said to my disease. "Just don't keep toying with me. Tell me when it's going to happen. Until then, I'm not slowing down for you. You can go to hell."

On 14 May I tried to end my life by taking an overdose. I was feeling too depressed about the future and didn't see any hope of anything getting better. I was taken to hospital where I stayed until 17 May. After being discharged, I went back to working where I could and tried to combat my illness with a healthy lifestyle. I exercised when I could. I had money coming in from consulting jobs and also from television work.

I had a contract on the Central Coast and decided to move there. It was while I was working there I met Jack. He was a project manager with the company I was contracted with. We got off on the wrong foot when he asked to see 'Melanie' one morning. I can't stand it when people get my name wrong, so I was not impressed. However, Jack and I were thrown together in the workplace and so were forced to get along. We soon became fast friends, and he said I could live at his place, so I moved in. Jack and I got along well and still do to this day. We know we can count on each other.

On 24 August 2004, I received the divorce papers, which set off a wave of terrible depression, but I battled on the best I could. A month later, I went back on my decision regarding not seeing my mother again. I agreed to meet her and my sisters at Macquarie Shopping Centre in Sydney for lunch. I was beginning to feel hatred for my mother, but I pushed that feeling down, still feeling that I owed her and my sisters another chance. That day, I tried again to connect with them. My mother saw the tattoo on my arm and made a disparaging remark.

My tattoo said *This Will Pass*. It had meaning for me, especially at such a painful time. I walked through that shopping centre in a fugue-like state. I knew in the pit of my stomach that I had to let go of them. They were not good for me. The more time I spent with them, the more their negative comments would lodge in my head. Added to that, not one of them acknowledged the pain I was in that day. They didn't mention anything about the divorce or ask how I was feeling or if I was coping. They talked amongst themselves most of the time. I felt invisible.

I realised that this time, *this* was it. I could never see them again.

Even though I knew not seeing them ever again was the right decision, I felt devastated. I just wanted a family who loved and accepted me. I was admitted to hospital with depression in September and stayed for a few days until I was stabilised and well enough to leave.

One afternoon, I received a phone call from my father. He rang to tell me that my sister Amanda had just been diagnosed with a similar condition to mine.

"She's having problems stepping up and down gutters," he said. "Poor Amanda."

"Yes, well," I said, "I live in a suburb where the gutters and kerbs are crazy, some high, some low, some uneven. You get used to it and find ways to negotiate them."

I didn't want to sound hard and unsympathetic, but my sister had shown no interest in my life or situation. I knew that my mother would be doing everything for her now that she was sick. She'd never once expressed any sympathy for me, and I certainly wasn't going to give her any.

"She has to have lots of cortisone injections," my father said.

"Yeah, well, so do I. I've had more cortisone injections than an injured rugby player and more Botox than a supermodel. Look, you just have to find a way of doing things. If you want to go for a walk, you have to train yourself not to look around. You've got to keep your head down and look at the pavement for cracks and bumps. She has to learn to do those things."

I didn't have the emotional energy to worry about her. Not long after that, Amanda rang.

"How long have I got before I end up like you?" she asked.

There was no asking about how I was going, what I had been doing, how I was managing or any other questions to do with my welfare. Despite her not being interested in my situation, I genuinely felt sorry for her because I didn't want anybody to go through what I was going through.

"I don't know," I said.

It was an honest answer. I decided I couldn't have any more contact with her either. I said goodbye and didn't mean just for the time being. I meant forever.

I had to find new doctors and health practitioners on the Central Coast. A doctor put me in touch with a psychologist to help me navigate all the physical and psychological changes that were happening in my life. I felt comfortable with Jenny straight away. I'd seen a lot of psychologists before, especially with the number of suicide attempts I'd had, but this woman was the first person with whom I felt a connection. In the past, when I'd seen a psychologist, it had usually been in response to a suicide attempt. The first concern was always to ensure I was safe and in a safe place for the short term. The psychologists in the hospital were compassionate, but because I only saw them for such a short time, there was no follow-up and therefore, no bond formed.

This time, it was different. At first, my sessions with my psychologist were taken up with my mental health assessment. It wasn't good. I was severely depressed, and I didn't want to accept my disease. I pushed down my emotions because I was so hurt, and I didn't want anyone to hurt me again. When I realised that I could trust her, I started to talk about my life, my marriage, my mother, and everything else that had gone on. I didn't know how to deal with all the hurt. I couldn't manage it or my health. In the early days, we focused on how to manage my feelings about my disease, but later, we started to talk about other aspects of my life. I wasn't used to telling strangers about personal issues. It wasn't the way I was raised. It still took me some time to open up, but I felt I could trust her once I did. I knew then that I was in for the long haul. I started telling her about my life. She listened and wasn't judgemental. Talking like this was a new experience for me. I came from a family that only meted out criticism; everything I did or said was wrong, so telling someone who didn't judge was refreshing. Even when I had been hospitalised for attempting suicide, I felt that I had done something awful and was inconveniencing all the people who were trying to help me.

I started to talk about my marriage. I was having trouble working out whether my marriage was real. It was very confusing. For the first time, I doubted whether my feelings for my ex-husband were real. Was it love? Was it something else? Did I even know what love was? I knew what it was like to want approval desperately, but approval wasn't the same as love. Did I get married to please my mother?

My psychologist, Jenny, had a way of drawing information out of me and then letting me sit with it. I had no way of knowing if what I had done over the past years was right or wrong. I had always believed that what my mother said about me was right, but at the same time, I couldn't put up with her comments as they were too hurtful. People raised in the atmosphere I was raised in have no signposts, red flags, or barometer with which to measure behaviour. We honestly don't know if what has been done to us is normal, abnormal, abusive, damaging or whether all families behave in the same way.

When I started to work with the psychologist, a transference of ideas began to wash over me, and it was, at first, all done by body language. For the first time, I encountered somebody who was saddened and shocked by my mother's treatment of me. The psychologist never came out directly and stated that she thought it was terrible or abusive or that she didn't deserve to be a mother. Sometimes, when I related an incident to her, she would breathe heavily and sit up a bit straighter, adjust her shirt and sit back with an expression that said it all. I would go away and think about that session over the next few days, and then suddenly, I would realise that what she was expressing was sympathy for me and disapproval regarding my mother's behaviour. It sounds so basic, but I wasn't good at recognising abuse as I was so used to it. I'd always been told I was selfish, and for the first time, I started to reject this idea. How could I be selfish when I'd done everything my mother had told me to do? How could I be selfish when I'd let my mother pick out my wedding date even though she knew I needed more time? How could I be the selfish one when I had invented an affair so that my husband would leave me even though he was the one cheating on me? I was supposed to be the selfish one, and yet my then-husband had abandoned me at a time when I was dealing with the most devastating diagnosis and a terrifying future. Added to that, I grieved the loss of happiness and the future that I may have had with the man who was my soulmate.

I continued to work with my psychologist as we unravelled my journey. It was difficult work, and I didn't see the results straight away, but I wanted to keep going as I felt that finally I was being listened to. It was only after I'd come out with statements about my mother and how I now saw her that the psychologist would say something. She let me work it out for myself. Even though this was happening, it still didn't lessen my hurt. It just explained where it came from. My psychologist helped me work through my feelings to be less confused. It was challenging to break the habit of a lifetime – the habit of believing that everything was my fault because that's what my mother had taught me. I came to see that I had to forgive myself. I deserved dignity and happiness. Saying those things and even realising them to be true still didn't mean that my thoughts would change overnight. It would take years of therapy, years of chipping away at my false fixed beliefs and replacing them with positive ideas that paid respect to the skills that saw me become so successful in my career. Years of brainwashing me into believing that I was inherently flawed could not be undone overnight.

Working with my psychologist also opened me up to accepting that the failed marriage wasn't all my fault. Formerly, even when James had hurt me, I always attributed the hurt to a fault in me. For the first time, I seriously considered the idea that it could take two to wreck a relationship or even one, but the one didn't necessarily have to be me. We both made mistakes. A man who shows no concern for his partner when she has been sexually assaulted and gets up to go to work the next morning as though nothing has happened clearly has something missing. James couldn't accept that we would never have children, and his way of dealing with it was to have an affair, which led me to break up the marriage. All that, instead of telling me he couldn't stay. It was such a big part of what he wanted for his life that he couldn't face a future without that part. I came to realise that it would never have worked.

I started to understand that my explanation of 'it's just the way she is' regarding my mother and also 'it's just how I am' in regard to myself didn't explain or help me at all. Over time, I began to see that 'the way she was' was not normal and that 'the way I was' was not healthy either. I had no yardstick with which to measure family behaviour. When I was growing up, the only barometer to family behaviour was television. There, some families were functional, and some were not.

I realised there had to be reasons for anyone's behaviour and that understanding these reasons, as painful as they were to look at, were the key to start getting better. I was immobilised with negative thoughts, and this kept me trapped. It would be a long time before I would begin to feel better, but I'd made a start. I told Jenny things I had never told anyone else. I had walked into a shop and walked out with an item without paying for it. I didn't understand why I did that. Feeling guilty, I punched myself in the face and effected a big, black eye. After many sessions with Jenny, she made me see that I wanted to inflict pain on myself by doing something I would never do. I needed to self-harm, and I wanted a reason. Feeling bad about myself wasn't enough. The act had nothing to do with the item itself. I neither needed it nor wanted it. It was simply a vehicle for an outcome. I had to forgive myself for this act, and I went back to the store and made up a story about why I had not paid for the item. I paid for it and walked out. I felt disgusted with myself, but in time, I was able to forgive myself. It was a massive step in my journey to be able to forgive myself. I'd never done it before.

Just because I was seeing a psychologist and working through some of my issues didn't mean that I instantly changed my behaviour. I came to see that my psychologist wouldn't tell me what was wrong or how to fix it, but instead, we'd talk about specific topics, and I would slowly come to my own conclusions. I was still self-harming and occasionally would still try to end my life.

I still didn't understand why my mother hated me so much. The rejection was sometimes too much to bear, and the pain was occasionally too much to live with. I now understood it was wrong, but I still didn't know why my mother was the way she was.

One night, I took some medication, pouring out two tablets into my hand, which was the usual dose. I had the urge to take three. Then I took four. Then five. Then six. I kept on going until the bottle was empty. Why not? I reasoned. It would put an end to it. There would be peace. Before I lay down, I rang a friend to say goodbye. Many people say that those who take an overdose and then ring someone don't really want to die. In my case, that's not true. When I take an overdose, I do want to go, but I always have to say goodbye first. A part of me wants to do things properly, and saying goodbye is important to me. I didn't want my friend to intervene, but she did and rang an ambulance. Another friend asked me a few days later why I wanted to end it all. I don't know, I told her. And I didn't. Sure, there'd be no more physical pain. There'd be no more depression. But why hadn't I succeeded? Was there a reason why I was still here?

As the months went by, more and more information about my family emerged. When I was asked about my reactions to some of the cruel behaviour and comments that were meted out to me as a child by my mother, the answer was easy. How did you feel at the time? I thought that I was a bad child. I was stupid. I had no common sense. I would never amount to anything. I was just a girl, so I couldn't do certain things. I was a burden on the whole family, especially my mother. I was always sick. I was a fruit loop. I ruined things for other people. Talking about how I felt was not difficult. My psychologist helped me to bring out my whole story. It took years, but over that time, I began to understand why I had put up with such abuse.

Why did you believe all of those things?

Because she was my mother, everything she said had to be right. Didn't it?

There lay the core of my problem. As children, we assume that the way our families behave and interact is normal. We have nothing to compare our families with until we reach a certain cognizance and can see the differences between how others are raised and how we were. I thought that my mother was the same as any other mother. I couldn't get angry with her. Why would I? She knew best. When I look back now, I see my family and relatives almost as a cult, with my mother as the leader. They were completely under her spell. She had that effect on everyone. And my husband fell under her spell as well. The Karen cult, I told my psychologist. James was weak at heart and couldn't stand up to her. He fell into line, and an unhealthy transference of her contempt for me happened and so affected how he related to me. The rest of the family mistreated me, and James joined the party.

My psychologist and I delved back into the past to all those occasions when my mother had made cruel and insensitive comments, comments that could and did damage a vulnerable child. When was this? Who was with you? Where were you? Where was your sister, your husband, your father?

It was a lightning bolt moment. It shocked me. I took a few seconds before I answered, realising something I had never realised before.

"My father was never in the room."

My mother had picked her times, manipulating the situation so that no one else overheard. It was always calculated. I was shocked. It took a long time for this revelation to sink in.

I also realised that my marriage was not based on love; it was based on approval. I had never had approval from anyone, and I desperately wanted it. Walking down the aisle that day, I searched the faces in the church for their approval. My mother approved of James; she told all her friends how good looking and intelligent he was, how hardworking, how genuine and how he fitted in with the family so well. It was almost as though she lusted after him. There was nothing sexual about her relationship with him, but the desire on her part to have him as part of the family was quite obsessive. She never talked about me to her friends unless it was to complain, but when it came to James, she always praised her 'amazing' son-in-law. I came to see that there had been three people in my marriage. I was trying to please both of them and never would reach their pinnacle of perfection.

All of this I processed over time, but it still didn't answer the question of *why* she was so hateful towards me.

———

For the next three years, from 2005 to 2008, I ploughed on. I was still living at my friend Jack's place. As far as driving was concerned, things only got worse. My body was deteriorating, and my eyesight problem continued to plague me. I was finding it difficult to turn my head around quickly if I needed to. I couldn't walk to and from my car. In May of that year, I was issued with a Mobility Parking Permit. I was now under the care of a professor. I liked him from the start. He was very frank with me. He told me that in the next two years, I would lose the use of my legs and then my arms.

"Can you look inside my head and see what's going to happen in the future?" I asked my professor. Can't you cut it open and do some repair work?"

He explained that it didn't work like that. All I could do was keep on taking the drugs and minimise falls by tailoring my environment to make every-day functioning easier. There were times when I wanted to scream and cry and simply walk away from my own body, especially when I was conscious of losing the ability to do something that I used to do and then had to process that loss. I had to let go and say goodbye to things I took for granted in another life.

I tried to be positive. When I had a fall, I'd take a photo of the bruise, particularly if it was my face that was injured, and I'd laugh at the photo of my rearranged appearance. My face was the only Picasso I'd ever have.

In 2005, I was offered work in two major centres in Sydney. I lived part-time at a girlfriend's house and part-time in my car. I couldn't drive from Gosford to Sydney every day, but I didn't have anywhere to live. Rents in Sydney were increasing, and I didn't have the finances to cover rent at the time. My car and I became the best of friends during this period. It wasn't ideal, but I made it my home for a while.

It was terrifying sleeping in the car. It was cold weather, so the windows were closed. I had all the doors locked. It wasn't good quality sleep. If I could get a park in the secured car park at work, I would stay the night there in my car. That car park was not accessible to the outside world once a person was in there. If not, I'd park at the King Street wharf. I'd get up early and go into the office for a quick shower or a wash in the bathrooms and then start work. I didn't want anyone to know I was sleeping in my car. It was too easy for people to find out that I was homeless if I had been sleeping in the office. My dignity was important to me. I knew my boss would have understood, but the boss above him certainly would not have understood.

Even living in a car, I was still a tidy freak. Everything had a proper place in the car. I configured the car so that everything was organised. I put the front seat down because it was more comfortable to sleep. I couldn't sleep in the back seat because my legs would have been dangling out the door. I borrowed an oversized jacket from a friend and put it in the boot of the car. I didn't want blankets in the back in case it looked like somebody was living in the car, and that might draw attention.

I'd iron all my clothes for the week at a friend's house and put them on hangers on the hook above the window. The goal was to wear black pants and five different shirts for the week. It was like a uniform, and it was easier to deal with. Gone were the days where I'd get up and think, 'Oh, what will I wear today?' It was difficult without a washing machine, so once a week, I'd go to a friend's place and use her washing machine. Here, I could have a long hot shower and wash my hair. I'd make sure I had a supply of clean underwear for the next week, and I'd wash other clothes as well. Sometimes, I'd just have to throw clothes away. It was very cold as it was winter, but I couldn't leave the car heater on all night. I wore thick socks and heavy jumpers. If my feet were covered, I'd feel safer.

As for hygiene, I bought some cheap washers I could use once and throw them out as there was nowhere for me to dry them. I'd make sure I didn't drink anything after a specific time in the afternoon, and I held on to the next morning if I had to go to the bathroom. Ice cream buckets with lids and toilet paper are a staple for those who are living in their car.

Once, I slept in the office as I'd taken a lot of medication. I woke up at my desk the following day. It was very stressful. I look back on that time and wonder how I survived it. I'd always work back so that I could stay in the office for as long as possible. The office had a TV, so I watched the news and other programs. Sometimes, I was the only person working back then. I'd wait and wait for others to leave, and they'd stay until late. They had wives and girlfriends and kids to go home to. They had warm beds and showers and food and all the conveniences that made life comfortable. It was almost like they didn't want to go home. It made me feel extremely frustrated with them. I felt like screaming. 'Go home; you don't know how lucky you are.'

I usually ate in the afternoon or early evening, and if no one was working back, I could clean my teeth and floss them in the bathroom. After I'd gone into my car, I wouldn't eat again. Sometimes, I'd go without food if it meant I could move the car into the secure car park.

Occasionally, my boss would send me to stay at his sister's place, which was empty at the time, but I couldn't stay there; there was baby paraphernalia everywhere. It set off something inside me: the pain of giving up my dream of having my own family.

When that contract ended, I moved back in with Jack. I was having trouble with my balance, and one morning, I fell forward onto a glass table and broke my leg. It was a hassle being in plaster for a while. I got some consulting work, and it went well. My stomach problems had started to re-occur, so I spent quite a bit of time at the doctor. I found out that my sister had had a baby. Although I was happy for her, I was sad at the same time. I would never live that dream. A few months later, I was depressed again when I found out at the end of 2005 that James had married. His second child was born a few months later. I did contract work throughout that year.

In 2006, I was still undertaking contract work, but my body was starting to deteriorate at a rapid pace. Co-ordination was becoming more difficult. I was insulted when James contacted me in March to ask if I would give him back the shares he had bought me as a present. I gave them back.

In October 2006, James sold the house we had bought together. His mother bought it but didn't tell her husband that she and James had gone half-half. I got nothing as I let him have it all. This was one of my biggest regrets. My low self-esteem and the fact that I blamed myself for not making him happy, coupled with my father's harassment about giving James money, saw me miss out on what was rightfully mine.

Although I was doing a great job with the contracts I had, I was worried about how long I would be able to keep up. My eyes were failing, and my movements were becoming more and more uncontrolled. I had to be mindful of keeping my eyes on the ground when walking because if I didn't, I'd have a fall. I still managed to go to work and social functions and went out with girlfriends.

I was offered some event work at a major centre in Sydney in December 2006. We were having a Santa arrival at the centre, so we all had a staff centre breakfast at six-thirty to prepare for the organisation for the day. The parents pay for the children to have breakfast with Santa, so there is much to organise: food, drink, catering, tables and chairs, bins, security, and transport. I was feeling exhausted from trying to keep on top of everything. It was all too much, and I felt the familiar black blanket of depression about to suffocate me.

On a Friday night, I decided to take my life, and I took an overdose of sleeping pills. I don't remember how I got to hospital, but that's where I woke up. My stomach was pumped. I stayed for a few hours and then discharged myself. I had a few hours' sleep, and then the alarm went off, and the morning began. I drove to work. People commented that I looked like shit and asked me if I was all right. My walls went up, and I told them I was fine. After the event, I helped clean up and then drove to Fox Studios to do an event there. This became my pattern. Overdose, get up and start again. Overdose, get up and start again. It went on for months. Hospital admission. See a psychologist. Discharge. And again, and again.

My body was now starting to break down at a furious pace. I couldn't keep up as physically I was falling apart.

I tried not to think about the future, but I was forced to do so when I was offered a big event – Carols in the Domain. This was the first event I had to turn down. I knew that I couldn't give it one hundred per cent and so, therefore, I couldn't do it at all. I was confident that if I stuffed anything up at a significant event, I would attempt suicide again. The company was a bit shocked when I told them that I couldn't come on board, but they understood. They offered me more money, but it wasn't about the money; it was about doing a great job, and I wasn't up for it. I was beginning to be unsteady on my feet.

"I'm taking over," said Cerebral Atrophy. "Not just yet, you're not," I replied.

Because I couldn't do big jobs, I took on smaller ones where I didn't have to put in so many hours of overtime. I felt unwell most of the time but ploughed on. As my body deteriorated, I was no longer able to work, and I stopped working full-time in December 2006. It was the end of my career, the end of a dream. It was one of the hardest decisions I've ever made, but I had to face the truth. I couldn't go on anymore. Doing so would have not only put my health in jeopardy but it would have meant doing a lousy job and letting people down.

I had a holiday in Fiji, paid for by the company I was working with. This was the last time I was able to work full-time.

"You can't ignore me now," said Cerebral Atrophy.

"I surrender," I told my disease. I had no energy to fight back anymore.

The decision to stop working full-time was devastating for me. For a long time, I had suppressed the knowledge that there would come a day when everything would change. Work gave me a purpose, a passion, a chance to use my skills and be creative and, of course, an income. It was good for my self-esteem, as well. It proved to the world that I wasn't those things that my mother said I was. It countered the negative ways I was brought up. It was my saviour. I was now unemployed. My doctors wrote the necessary reports for a disability pension. I had sunk into a bad depression but battled on, occasionally doing some consulting work if I could manage it. The end of 2006 came with other people's happy news; my friend Cam was pregnant, my boss and his wife had just had a baby, and my sister-in-law and brother also had a baby. Everybody had what I most wanted. I felt I was in hell. I was genuinely happy for my friends, but the news hit me in the guts.

Throughout 2007 I managed to do some consulting work part-time. I was still working with my psychologist, and when I wasn't working, I was trying to manage my illness. I was now catching trains and buses and doing a lot of walking when I could as driving was just too difficult. I did some event management for the Royal Easter Show and a few black-tie events. I was now seeing quite a few specialists and therapists. It took up a lot of my time. I was head-hunted by a major company to do some work and managed to do it, although I was feeling exhausted.

It was in 2008, while I was still living with Jack, that the deterioration of my body became very serious. I was experiencing quite a few falls. Falling became a daily event as the months wore on. This was a new, very terrifying experience. It was like my mind and body were not talking to each other. Like they didn't belong together. It was a dark place to be. I knew what I wanted to do, but when I went to do it, my body just refused to do what I wanted. Bruises were a common sight on my body. I broke my hand and then two ribs. I had some more tests, and when I next saw the specialists, they had terrible news for me.

"The MRI has revealed that the cells on both the right and left side of your brain are deteriorating further," they told me.

There was nothing I could say. There was no cure, only drugs that could manage the symptoms of the disease and physical therapy. I nodded dumbly. It was bad enough that physically, I would fall apart, but I was terrified of my brain going as well.

I still talked to my disease and tried to laugh when I fell over. It worked some of the time, but there were days when the slightest of things could send me into a pit of depression and despair. On the day I found out that James had taken his first holiday with his new wife and family, I was in the city with a girlfriend. I was trying not to let that information get me down. The bunch of keys I was carrying fell out of my hands and went down a covered stormwater drain. To most people, this would be frustrating and an inconvenience, but for me, depressed and growing more depressed as my body fell apart, it was the last straw. It felt like the whole world was conspiring against me to make life as miserable and as difficult as possible when it already was no picnic. I had moved out of Jack's and had to find a place to live. I completely fell apart emotionally and was admitted to Mosman Private Hospital.

13. Sea Change

After the stint in Mosman Private's psychiatric ward, I decided to move back to Sydney, and I took a flat in Bondi. It was 2009; I was on my own, trying to make a life, juggling my health and some consulting work, and trying to get over the past events and the hurt that my family had inflicted on me. I didn't expect that anything else could happen that hadn't already happened, and so I was unprepared for what happened one night when I ran out of milk.

I knew the shop on Bondi Road would still be open. It wasn't late, not even eight o'clock. As I was leaving the shop, I felt a tap on my shoulder, and when I turned around, I recognised a family friend.

"Hi, Melissa, good to see you," he said.

I felt uneasy, thinking that he'd probably heard all about my marriage break up and the affair.

"So, how are you?"

I told him I was doing all right. He said he had been at a meeting not far from where we were. He asked me where I was living, and I told him.

"Great. You got milk? I'll get the biscuits, and we'll catch up at your place."

I asked him whether it would be better if we went to a local place to have a cup of tea or coffee, but he said he'd love to see where I lived.

"I know you don't speak to your parents anymore, but I want you to know you're not alone."

I reminded myself that he was a family friend. I didn't want to hear about my parents or siblings, so I thought I'd concentrate on his family when we talked.

I opened the door to my apartment. He wasted no time. As soon as I opened the door, he pushed me into the room, grabbed me and pushed himself up against me.

"What are you doing?" I cried.

"I've wanted to do this with you for a long time," he said.

His voice was aggressive. I thought I might faint. I begged him not to do anything.

"I know you want it," he said. "You had an affair. You're up for anything, and I know how much you love sex."

"Please, stop. Please don't do this." He became even more aggressive.

"When I heard how much you loved sex, I had a hard-on like you wouldn't believe. I'm gonna give it to you like you've never had it before."

I struggled against him, but it was no use. He completely overpowered me. The torture went on for nearly an hour. At one point, he told me I was too tight. After he had finished assaulting me, he got dressed. I had his sweat on my body. I could still feel his breathing. I felt repulsed and disgusted.

"Remember, I've known you since you were little, and I know your parents really well. If you tell anybody or say anything about this, who do you think people are going to believe?"

I scrubbed myself in the shower and went to bed, but I stayed awake the whole night, crying, reliving his rough hands, his breath, his smell. My entire body was sore. I felt like I wanted to die. His words were like a loop tape in my head.

Who do you think they'd believe?

It was surreal. After the Canberra attack, it didn't seem possible that it could happen again, and this time it was so much worse. And with someone who'd known me since I was a child.

I knew there would be no sympathy for me if I told my family. I knew what my mother's response would be. He was a married man with children. I was a slut, a worthless piece of dirt. And I deserved it. I didn't go to the police. The voice in my head loomed up, telling me I was useless. I imagined the police wouldn't believe me either. I had to handle it on my own.

One of my old bosses offered me some part-time work in the pubs he owned, so I worked as a hostess in the poker machine area, encouraging the patrons to have a go and a drink at the same time. Part of my job was to go across the road into a competitor's pub and encourage people to go into my boss's pub. I became friends with one of my co-workers, Glenn. Glenn and I had regular Scrabble competitions, and we were both very determined to beat the other.

Our owner had seven pubs, five in Sydney and two in Newcastle. As I lived there rent-free, I did the cleaning, which was very tough work. I'd vacuum the downstairs area and then go upstairs and vacuum the gaming area. I'd clean the bathrooms downstairs and upstairs, put the furniture back in its rightful place, empty the ashtrays and pick up rubbish and empty glasses. The chefs cleaned the kitchen, but even if the kitchen was closed and they had cleaned up for the night and were preparing to go home, they would cook me a meal if they saw me come in. I was very grateful for that. It was one less thing to do when I was feeling run down as my body deteriorated. I went to the pubs in Newcastle quite often, worked a shift in the gaming room, and drove home. My room at the pub was upstairs and fortunately had its own shower and toilet. It had a bed and a desk. If I wanted to wash and dry clothes, I had to use the machines downstairs that belonged to the pub. The noise from downstairs filtered into my room, and so did the cigarette smoke, which I found revolting. I had to keep the windows closed all the time as my room was above the outside smoking area. Sometimes, a drunken patron would try to get into my room, and at those times, I was pretty scared.

The work was quite enjoyable as I wasn't under any stress, and I got to chat with the patrons. I now had some money, a job, and a place to live, but despite all that, my depression was worsening with each passing day. I had hit an all-time low. Every few weeks, there was some part of my body that was not obeying, and I dreaded anything new I had to cope with. I knew that the disease was increasing, but I was trying not to think about it. Visits to the neurologist were increasing.

In addition to the pub work, I also worked for a friend of mine who was an event organiser. I liked the black-tie events best but didn't like the uniforms. We had to wear very short dresses and long white boots. I sometimes worked at rave parties, selling cigarettes. I don't know if the work was legal because the merchandise was not on display, and patrons had to come up and ask for it. I don't even know if the events were legal. They were held far from the city, and it took ages to drive there. There was a lot of drinking and drug-taking, and the noise level was horrendous. The patrons would scream over the music, and I would scream back. In the morning, my ears would be ringing and sore, and my throat felt like I'd swallowed gravel.

I got the same sort of work at drag races, and once again, the noise levels were terrible. I needed the money, and working was good for my self-esteem. On occasions, I had to don a costume. I've been Sexy Girl, Tweedy Bird, Rudolph the Red-Nosed Reindeer and Santa's Elf. I smiled and made small talk. I went home exhausted.

As each day passed, I felt I was losing control. My conversations with my disease were not as bolshy as they once had been. They were now more of an entreaty.

"Please don't progress anymore. Not just yet. Let me have more time. I've got more to do. Don't progress. I'm begging you."

Cerebral Atrophy smirked and twisted the knife.

"Not gonna' do it. I'm progressing, and you're regressing."

There was nothing solid and secure in my life anymore. I missed James, even though I knew the marriage wasn't right for me. I wanted to be strong, but I didn't feel it. I wanted a supportive family, but I didn't have one. My weight had plummeted to a size four. I didn't see much hope anywhere. I looked around my tiny flat. The kitchen doubled as a storage room, ironing room, and clothing rack room. The sexual assault, on top of everything else, confirmed in me that there didn't seem much point to living at all, and so on 14 May 2009, I decided to end it all. I was still self-harming but decided to take pills. Clonazepam, a benzodiazepine, is my drug of choice. They come in a bottle of two hundred. I had once taken a whole bottle in a previous attempt, and it hadn't worked, so I took two bottles this time. Clonazepam is a drug used for treating seizures, panic and akathisia. Akathisia is a movement disorder. It is characterised by restlessness, particularly in the legs, and can also affect mood.

I was pretty much out of it as soon as I finished swallowing the second bottle. I had become quite good at ingesting large amounts of tablets with small amounts of water. I could take one hundred little pills with one gulp of water.

After I had swallowed two hundred pills, I texted Glenn and other friends to say goodbye. He called and told me to hang on and that he was on his way. I remember the fracas outside my door as I slipped into unconsciousness. Glenn must have called the pub. I heard the kitchen cooks running down the hallway, shouting. I heard the smash of glass and wood as they kicked the door in. I had locked the door but remembered the pub had keys to my flat, so I wondered why they just didn't unlock it. After that, I blacked out completely. I found out later that the kitchen boys had called an ambulance, and Glenn had come with me to hospital. He told me later that the bottles were on my bed, so the paramedics knew what I had taken but didn't know the amount.

Some nurses are not very nice to those who attempt suicide. That day, I got one of those. She poured plastic cups of charcoal down my throat. Every time I tried to resist, she told me that I was making it worse for myself. It was very messy. The charcoal goes everywhere, then there's the vomiting, then the tablets come up, and more charcoal is poured. I know the staff have to do their job to save a life, and they have to act quickly, so I suppose there's no time for sympathy or niceties. After the procedure, I was not allowed to be alone. A staff member accompanied me to the bathroom. Looking back, I am grateful for the nurses doing their job.

After a short stay in a general ward, I was moved to the psychiatric ward. As soon as all my documentation was completed, I was locked in a ward. A nurse came in, patted me down and went through my belongings. She showed me to my room and told me where I could find the bathroom.

As soon as I was alone, I sat on the bed and cried. There were no locks on the doors, so anyone could walk in when they wanted. The room was small; it had a single bed and a bedside table with no drawers. As I looked around the room, I noticed a small patch of blood on the wall behind the bedhead on the bedside table and a few more blood smears around the bedroom. It made me feel sick. I knew I was on suicide watch as I wasn't left alone for very long. A nurse came with me when I used the bathroom, and another nurse brought my dinner into my room.

"You're a failure. You can't even kill yourself properly," said Cerebral Atrophy. On the first night, I didn't socialise with the other patients. In the morning,

I asked to have a shower, and I was advised I would be provided with a towel. All my belongings were locked up. I asked for my handbag as I had a few items in there that I could use to freshen up. I was allowed this only after the bag had been checked. My clothes had been taken away the night before. Friends and family could bring things in for patients except for certain items. Dressing gowns with chords were not allowed. No disposable razors, sharp objects or anything that could be used to self-harm.

I was shocked that the shower cubicles didn't have locks on the doors. The nurse told me that if the door is closed, it means somebody is in there. After my shower, I wandered around the ward for a while, but I found it very confronting. There were some very ill people there, and I crept around, not wanting to draw attention to myself. I asked for a book, which was in my handbag, and was given it. One patient in the ward asked for something out of his bag every ten minutes. The nurses kept telling him he didn't need anything and to sit down and relax. I sat and read and drank lots of tea. I saw a psychologist every day I was there.

By the third day there, I spoke to other patients. A lot had many scars, which I know were self-inflicted. Several patients were crazy, and delusional, and others talked to themselves and hit themselves. Some would just sit and stare at me. I found this quite disturbing. I didn't want to spend the rest of the weekend locked up. A doctor came to see me and informed me that he would like me to stay, and he would re-assess me the following week. I told him I wanted to go home. He tried to talk me into staying, and I became so scared that I mentioned ringing my lawyer. I didn't have a lawyer, but it was the only thing I could think of to say. Because I wasn't scheduled, I could leave when I wanted to. One of the nurses approached me and said that I could arrange for somebody to pick me up before the staff changeover. A friend came to pick me up, I signed myself out, collected my bag, and we jumped into a cab. I couldn't bear the thought of being locked up.

Back at home, I began to play games that would keep my brain active as I was terrified of losing my mental faculties. I played Scrabble and other games, which would hopefully keep my grey matter intact enough to get through the day.

In September 2009, my legs decided they didn't want to work. I woke up one morning, and I couldn't get out of bed without help. This was very depressing, but I learned how to hoist myself up and start my day. My legs were weak, but I could still walk. I used self-talk; talking to my illness and getting angry with it, and not myself, helped.

"Okay, you've now got my legs, but that's all you're getting for a while."

"I'll get more as time goes on," said Cerebral Atrophy.

"You might, but for now, that's all you're getting. So piss off, and let me get on with it."

Visits to the neurologist increased, and the number of drugs increased as well.

Palm Beach was my next move in 2010. My disability pension covered my rent and food, and because I didn't go out much, I was all right and just got by. I wasn't doing any work at all as I just wasn't well enough. I continued to do mind puzzles and Scrabble. I was sharing the place with my friend, Julia, who was going through a nasty divorce settlement and another friend. Julia's ex-partner was making the divorce process very difficult, and she was drinking quite a lot to manage her stress. I was trying to help her. The house was quite big and had three levels.

Julia had the top level, which had a walk-in wardrobe and an ensuite with a spa bath. The bath was round. The house had a pool and a view of the lake. The house was undergoing renovations. My part of the house was in the basement. Usually, a boat was kept there, but it suited me for the time being. The basement was also being renovated, and eventually, there would be an ensuite there. In the meantime, I used the bathroom on the second level. In the basement, there was a roller door leading to the outside. Sometimes it would simply roll up on its own, exposing me in my bed to anyone who happened to be in the back garden. It usually happened at night, at two or three in the morning. I didn't know anything about roller doors, but when it happened, I got a broom and pulled on a cord so I could control the door.

It was a very harmonious household. We had fun as well. Tuesday night was lobster night at the local club, and sometimes we had dinner at the golf club. The house had a pool and a lovely garden. While there, I taught a friend how to drive, and she succeeded in getting her licence. One of my other friends hadn't done her taxes for four years. As far as her tax was concerned, everything was in a mess, with paperwork all over the place and no organisation at all. It was a big job, but it was something I was good at. I put her documents in years, then put everything on the computer for her accountant, which she didn't have, so I told her to get one. I was able to send all documentation to her accountant, who said he was happy with my work! I helped Julia with the paperwork and organisation for her impending divorce. I was fond of her, but sometimes, I couldn't disguise my irritation with her because of her heavy drinking. The boot of her car was full of empty bottles, mostly spirits. There were full and half bottles on the passenger seat in her car, with a cup. Sometimes, she'd even mix wine with bourbon and coke. Unsurprisingly, she went DUI and lost her licence. I knew that it would be almost impossible for her to stop drinking unless she got professional help and admitted she had a problem, which she wasn't going to do. I got into her car and drove to a nearby shopping centre one afternoon. There were huge industrial bins at the back. I parked the car next to the bins and took out all the bottles of vodka and other spirits. It took a while, but a thousand dollars' worth of alcohol went straight into the bins. People were staring at me, but I didn't care. A few times, I had to ring the police because she got into the car, very drunk, and thought she could drive. This got her into more trouble. Because she couldn't drive, she started getting alcohol delivery. One afternoon, a delivery came to the door. I looked at the receipt – $1,647.93. She'd paid for it, but I put it in my car, and the next day, I went to see the people who had supplied it and had a talk with them. I told them about the lost licence and the havoc her drinking was having on everyone. I expected them to tell me where to go and that it was none of my business, but they were very understanding, and we came to an agreement about how much they could deliver.

One night, she was very drunk and declared she was going to cook steak for me and a friend. She put the steaks on the grill for a few seconds, turned them over and told us they were done. She served up the rarest, bloodiest steak I have ever seen. Reluctantly, we forced small bits of steaks down, as we knew if we didn't eat them, she would have had a full-blown temper tantrum. We siphoned off the meat to the dogs. In the end, I gave up trying to help her. It was frustrating and sad to see someone destroy their life by choice when I had no choice. It did my head in to see people destroying themselves by their choices when I had never done what they had done, and yet something had been thrust upon me, and there was nothing I could do about it. I'd tried my best with Julia, even trying to help repair the rift between her and her children, but I didn't have the energy to continue.

These were things I could do as I could manage them from home (and car) and so even though I felt constantly run down, I kept my brain alive. I pushed my illness down. I spoke nicely to it at times.

"Let me have this time in this house, near the beach, just for a while before you make it worse. I'll never have this again. To listen to the waves and watch the sunset over the water is something I value so much. Show me some kindness, just for a while. I know you have to do it, but please do it slowly."

I knew my illness was a progressive disease, but I was trying to use reverse psychological tactics. One of my biggest fears was the thought that I would lose my mental faculties altogether. It was genuinely terrifying. Sometimes, I'd forget something, and then I'd wonder whether if I was just like most people who can't remember the name of someone or a place they'd been to or a date on which something happened or whether it was the disease creeping up on my memory, slowly eroding my recall of the past. My brain had always been so sharp; now, it felt like the edges were blunt. I had to keep it alive. I had to keep it contained and not let it fray at the edges.

My brain was kept active by also managing the problem of the house for the owner-builder and his partner. He had never attained certification on the house. Because he wanted to sell it, he needed it to be certified. That meant that certain things had to be done. If he'd sold it as it was, they would have lost quite a bit of money. He handed the job over to me. I knew a bit about building codes from my time in the shopping centre industry, but residential was another thing. Over time, I learned enough to understand what I needed to do. The owner was happy to let me take over the management, and I learnt new skills and even got to hire and fire people. Builders were employed to fix any problems, and if I wasn't satisfied, I'd fire them and hire new ones. It was fun spending someone else's money, but I also took the job seriously. The owners always had my back. Occasionally, there would be heated discussions with builders. I got the feeling that some didn't like it when confronted with a female who knew all about building codes and regulations.

The first thing I did was to buy three birdhouses for the backyard because the council were encouraging residents to attract birds into the area. They were very specific about locations and sizes. We were told that having the bird houses would lead to quicker certification. A council inspector had to come out to listen to the pool motor, and the stairs had to be fixed as some of them were out, and the pool had to be fenced. The garden and the steps leading down to it had to be reconfigured as the top of the steps was too close to the pool, and somebody (or a reckless teenager) could have fallen (or dived) from the steps into the pool. Over the four years that I lived there, I got the house into shape, and the owner was compliant with all the regulations. It was a proud moment as I felt I had achieved something.

I had organised some work for Julia and on her second morning in the new job I wanted to make sure she was up in time and wouldn't be late. I got out of bed, went to her part of the house, and called her name. She was awake. Satisfied that she was up and ready, I walked to one of the bathrooms on the second level to have a shower. There were two tiled steps to negotiate and a corridor with a pebbled mat at the bottom. It was one of those mornings when the disease just decided to play up. My legs decided to give way just as I opened the door. I clutched at the balustrade but fell heavily down the steps, blacking out. When I came to, I felt pain in my legs as they were twisted, and I couldn't get up. My face was firmly planted in the pebble mat, but I managed to call out for help. I could hear Julia calling back to me.

"I'm here. I've fallen."

"Where's here?"

"The steps," I told her.

"Which steps?" she asked. "This house is full of steps!" she shouted.

She managed to find me and helped me up. It was then that I tasted blood in my mouth and felt the pain in my face. My friend helped me onto the bed, where I lay down while the pain in my face got worse. Both my eyes were turning black. One of the workers who had come to do the renovations arrived then. He helped Julia get me up and into her car. Julia told him to run up the driveway and stop the traffic so she could quickly get the car out onto the main road. We went to a local doctor, who told me I had a broken jaw and nose.

I couldn't talk that much as everything hurt. Fortunately, I hadn't broken my legs or ankles or anything else. I needed to let the swelling on my face go down before the hospital could wire up my jaw and fix up my nose. We then drove to the pharmacy to get the painkillers prescribed by the doctor. I looked at my face in the car mirror while I waited for Julia, and it was not a pretty sight. Blended food was all I could put in my mouth, and everything liquid was done through a straw.

Julia took me home and then left for work. She had called the company and told them what had happened. It wasn't easy to eat and drink for the next few months. I had x-rays, and finally, when the swelling had gone down, I was sent to hospital to have my jaw wired and nose fixed. I had to do jaw exercises, and I found it difficult to open my mouth. Some food was off the menu. After a time, solid food was back on the menu as my jaw repaired. It was six months before I could eat steak. The swelling on my chin took a month to go. My eyes went through a rainbow of colours. I had to sleep on my back for eight months and take a lot of pain medication. To this day, my jaw aches in the colder months, and it also clicks sometimes when I talk. I still can't open my mouth very wide.

Despite what had happened with the fall, living in Palm Beach was a happy time for me. My body continued to break down, but I had the support of good friends. As time wore on, I noticed Julia's drinking was becoming worse. She was now becoming aggressive when she was drunk. I stayed there for three years until 2012. By that time, Julia's drinking escalated to the point where she became quite unstable. One night, in a drunken rage, she got a knife out and threatened to kill me. I couldn't run, but I walked as fast as possible in my wobbly state to my car; however, she was faster than me and caught up with me. She rammed my head against my car. I managed to catch onto one of her arms as she lashed out at me, and I bit her finger. The police came, but it was her word against mine. I told the police that pretty soon she would break down and cry, and that prediction came true. The police looked at me, and I told them I didn't want to press charges. She would become maudlin and beg forgiveness, but I was done living with her. We remained friends, but I made it clear that I couldn't share a place with her anymore. I understood she had an addiction to alcohol. As long as I wasn't living with her, we got along quite well.

I was so tired of moving; the thought of it made me feel ill, but I needed a more permanent place. I was reading a lot and trying to do some walking every day. Julia and I started puppy-sitting, which was a lot of fun. Julia then did something that has brought much joy into my life. She bought me a puppy. I christened him Ughboot. He's the most beautiful companion for me.

There were more changes ahead after I moved out of Palm Beach. I was no longer able to bring in enough income to support myself in private rental, so I was given a place in public housing. This was very hard for me to come to terms with. Once, I had been a homeowner. I wasn't a snob; it's just that I never imagined myself having to go into Housing. At first, I was very negative about this. I had lost my career and my own home and survived on a disability pension, and there was no other option but to get Housing. If any good has come out of that, it is that formerly, I had some prejudiced attitudes about people in public housing. I have some beautiful and supportive friends in both public and private housing. I never thought I'd end up in public housing, but I quickly realised that it is irrelevant where you live; it's what's in a person's heart that is important.

The first place I moved into was a private house, subsidised by the government in St Peters in Sydney's inner west. I had two housing places to look at. Jack came with me to get the keys to the first place. It was shocking, and I couldn't believe they were willing to let people live like this, but, as Jack was a builder, he could see the possibilities and told me to take it. So, I did. Between packing and cleaning, we were utterly exhausted. I packed and cleaned the old place, and I helped clean the new place. Jack was there as much as he could be. He pretty much cleaned the whole place. He then started repainting it. He painted it three times in six years, and I even got approval to paint the outside. Jack did that as well. Jack and Glenn moved all the heavy stuff across and into place, and I would bring boxes every time I came over. I was finally in the housing place. Jack tacked sheets to cover the windows until we could go shopping and buy blinds and curtains. The place needed a bathroom cabinet and various other things.

During that time, in 2013, at St Peters, I struggled with the challenges my body presented me with. Every day was now difficult as the disease set in and caused havoc with my arms, legs, eyes, speech, gait, and memory. I stayed there for a year, then the landlord wanted the premises back, so I had to leave. The place had stairs, and I had a problem with that, so I didn't mind moving. The Department of Housing found me a place in Glebe in Sydney's inner west in 2014. My grandfather once owned many properties in Glebe, so I felt connected to it. I have made good friends in Glebe, and my dog loves it too. I ploughed on through 2015 and 2016, doing the best I could with further deterioration happening.

In 2016, I spent some time in a rehabilitation hospital. The hospital had rung to tell me there was a bed available, but I had to be in there by no later than three o'clock that day, or the placement would go to another patient. It was already ten. I assured her I'd be there, and I was. The hospital was a little depressing – white clinical walls, hospital corners, laminate flooring, a cupboard, a bedside cabinet and a table on wheels. On the upside, I had a private room, which meant I had my own bathroom. There was a lounge chair, which faced looking out the window to Darling Street.

I started unpacking and was then advised that this room was probably only temporary, and I could be moved at any time, hopefully to another private room at any time. Until that happened, I made the room as comfortable as possible. My timetable was taped to the whiteboard opposite my bed. I started at 9 am the next day. Breakfast was at 8 am; afternoon tea was at 3.00 pm; dinner at 5.00 pm, and the evening snack was served at 7.00 pm. Scheduled eating was something I certainly wasn't used to. I went to bed early on the first night and was up early, showered and dressed when my food arrived, followed by a nurse who took my blood pressure, drew some blood, took my temperature and then gave me an injection in my stomach. I was told that blood pressure, blood taken, and pulse readings were done hourly, and the injection was to be given every morning. I was beginning to dread the program. I took a look at the therapy room. It was huge. Two parallel bars ran down the middle of the room. Different types of equipment stood mainly against the walls. Fit balls sat on racks, so patients didn't trip over them. A mirrored ceiling-to-floor cupboard housed all the therapists' tools at one end of the room.

I was moved to another room. I can only describe it as isolated. Room thirty was right at the other end of the rehab floor and the very last room. It was big, with a sofa and coffee table at the beginning of the room, then a lot of space before the room started. I felt quite teary as I surveyed the room, but I had no time to feel sorry for myself. It was time to unpack again before my next session in twenty minutes. At my next rehab session, I had a fall, and it left me feeling quite deflated. I had yet another fall soon after, but this was because of another patient. The patients all used the parallel bars at the same time. Someone could be using the inside when another patient was using the outside. It worked most of the time, but on this day, the patient in the middle rattled the bar as I positioned my hands on it for additional safety if needed. The movement knocked me flying, and I hit a chair, which moved as I was going down. The therapists stopped what they were doing to help me, but I just kept falling. There was nothing anyone could do. Finally, the floor stopped me. The therapists came running while the man who rattled the bar was still going through his sets.

Back in the isolation room, the nurses greeted me. "We're moving you," one of them said.

In the space of a couple of hours, I was now in room nineteen, opposite the nurses' station. I had packed and unpacked three times in one day. I was finally back in a room with a view and a lounge chair to sit on to look at that view. I felt alone and would spend most of my spare time with the door closed or sitting at the window looking out at the world. It gave me a sense of peace, however.

The peace didn't last long. I was moving again to another room, this time to a four-bedroom where I was told I'd be near the window. As I packed my things for the umpteen time, I found my bed was number one, and I was nowhere near the window. The room was number twenty-four. It was full and had two bathrooms, one with just a toilet and the other a shower room. I was doing my best to accept my situation. The room was certainly uninviting: four beds, two on each wall facing the other two on the opposite wall. I pulled my curtains around so I didn't have to see the other patients, but unfortunately, I could hear everything. I unpacked while crying. My lunch came. I turned away.

Snoring, farting, screaming, complaining and the continuous conversations of the nurses trying to understand the older patients' requests. There was no peace in the new room. I was the only patient in the room under seventy. The two older women in the room talked to each other in a language I could not understand. I didn't have a problem with other languages; the problem person was in a bed at the top of the room on the right-hand side, and the other was at the bottom of the room on the left-hand side. Hence, they had to shout to be heard, and the conversations continued for a very long time at a very high volume. I guess it hadn't occurred to anyone to place them close together as they were obviously from the same ethnic background, but perhaps there was a reason they were separated.

A nurse came to show me the toilet and shower room. I looked at the bathroom, and a feeling of despair welled up inside. Hair in the sink, the toilet not flushed, towels and dirty wet wipes on the floor, personal belongings left everywhere. I couldn't cope with it. Cloistered behind my curtains, I burst into tears. I couldn't stomach eating anything and had to use the staff bathroom as I refused to use the patients' bathroom. The nurses were very compassionate and understood completely. Once again, I packed my belongings and was moved back to room nineteen. I positioned my chair and looked out the window, hoping this was my last time unpacking.

My rehab specialist came in to update me.

"You now have a speech pathologist, a nutritionist, a physiologist and I would like you to meet a new neurologist. The neurologist will be back on Monday, so you will spend this weekend here as you have rehab and other sessions booked; then, after meeting the new neurologist, you can go home on Monday."

Monday came, but the new neurologist was a no-show. My rehabilitation professor called past to make sure I'd met the new neurologist, and having told him I hadn't, he arranged the meeting for the next day.

"It's called The American Sobriety Test. Close your eyes, walk in a straight line with one foot in front of the other."

I can't do it; I told the new guy when we finally met. I meant I literally couldn't. He promised me he would be right there to catch me if I fell. The floor had a hard surface. I fell.

"Oh! You really can't do that one!"

He helped me up. I confirmed that I was all right. I felt embarrassed. We made an appointment to see me in his offices, and he continued on his way. A sharp pain in my right hand soon overtook the pain from falling on my bottom. Red and swollen, I wondered if it was broken. I landed on it when I fell. After being administered pain killers, the nurses sent me down for an x-ray. Nothing broken. Just a lot of bruising.

My rehabilitation professor came to see me the morning I was leaving to ensure everything was organised and that all my follow-up appointments had been made and confirmed. He sat at the end of my bed and said the one thing I had never expected.

"Let's get you working again."

Working. That word had a particular meaning for me. Power. Perfection.

A leader in my field. Commitment to excellence. An Inspiration to others in the field. Power dressing. Mentoring to others. The words 'let's get you working' now took on another meaning. I couldn't go back to work as I had done before. I might be able to assist or volunteer, but I could never again reach the great heights of my career as I had known it. I expected more of myself. Now I had to rest. Now, I could not simply pick up that bag or folder in case I fell. Now, people couldn't count on me. I'm limited, I told myself. Limited. If I could have walked away from my own body, I would have.

Something good came out of rehab, however. When the staff introduced me to the pool, I wasn't sure how I'd go. Once in the water, I was amazed at how much movement I seemed to have without the pain. It felt fantastic. I began to walk and then run in the water. I was exhilarated and started to dance in the water. It didn't hurt, and I felt I didn't care who saw me dancing in the water. I was beyond feeling self-conscious, beyond wondering what others thought, beyond wondering if my body was going to betray me at any moment. I simply didn't care. And so, I danced in the water as though there were a melody, rhythm, and words. I felt completely liberated. As I was getting out of the pool, I completely forgot that I couldn't do certain things, so I lunged for a towel on the rack and almost fell flat on my face. In the water, I had felt invincible.

—

A letter arrived in 2017, telling me I may not be eligible to stay in public housing. I rang the Department of Housing and got the usual run around: the person in charge was at a meeting, they'll ring you back, no I can't tell you anything. No one ever rings back; they're always at meetings, on leave, or have had a promotion, and yes, of course, they'll pass that message on. I managed to speak to someone who told me that to get another six-year lease, I had to get my doctors and specialists to provide documentation that proved I was eligible. This sort of thing is enough to tip people like me over the edge. I am already on a disability pension, and to be on that pension in the first place, there had to be evidence of my illness, information they already have. Do they think that suddenly I have miraculously recovered? Do they think I can resume a career so I don't need housing anymore? The stress of having to run around procuring information that they already have, making calls to my doctors and specialists to write reports that confirm my illness is draining and stressful. People living with chronic, deteriorative diseases do not need bureaucratic nonsense like this to tie up their time and make them anxious. It is sadly ironic; I'm dying, and yet they are worried about my next six-year lease. Added to this, The Department of Housing had only just made modifications to my home. Railings and bars were fitted, the bathroom was completely re-done, and the kitchen had some modifications. Therefore, the Department would have all that information about my disability. It is a case of the right hand not knowing what the left hand is doing. A friend contacted my local member, who was fantastic. Within days,

Housing fixed the problem, and I didn't have to prove that I needed housing. It makes people acutely anxious when these problems crop up. I understand why some people couldn't cope with the Robodebt scandal; it pushes people like us over the edge when we are already dealing with so many other issues.

Trying to get accurate information about the National Disability Insurance Scheme when it came in was just as frustrating. I filled in some paperwork to do with the NDIS, and I heard nothing for a long time. I rang and was told that my paperwork had been lost. They eventually found it, but that situation caused undue stress for me.

As time passes, my specialist is arming me with knowledge. He told me that in time, as my body deteriorates, there will be certain things that will become increasingly difficult. When I was first told that I had this disease, I accepted what I was told: that, in time, my body would start to fall apart. I accepted this because it was not happening to me at that stage. When things did start to go wrong, I was incredibly angry. Simple activities were becoming more difficult as time passed. I needed to go to rehab to build up my body and learn other ways to do the things that most of us take for granted every day. A friend had seen me walking up to the shops and told me the day after that he had seen me. I asked him why he hadn't said hello or waved. He said he could tell I was concentrating hard on the pavement, my head down, watching every step. He knew that if he had yelled out, I certainly would have fallen.

Small things that in the past had never bothered me now started to take on a new anxiety level. I began doing jigsaws for brain maintenance and then went on to various puzzles. Lately, the puzzles are just too hard, so I've gone back to doing jigsaws. I was doing one recently and feeling quite satisfied with it until I realised that the sky was all wrong. I just couldn't get the right piece to fit; I tried to configure the shape in my head and search for a matching piece, and the more I tried, the more anxious I became. It really pissed me off. People don't understand. It's just a jigsaw, they say. It's such a small thing, but to people who have an illness like me, it's a huge thing. It's the meaning behind it; it's about deterioration. It's about control. Even small things we can control give us a sense that there are still things we are in charge of. It is not our bodies controlling us. Not being able to fit in a jigsaw piece can completely undo us. It can do our heads in, bring on an episode of depression and sometimes lead to the decision to end it all.

"Let me just do the sky right, please. Just the sky, I will leave the rest. You can take over, but leave me the sky so I know I'm not completely losing everything. It's not a lot to ask. Just the sky. Please."

Cerebral Atrophy was mean that day. Not even the sky. I sank into depression. "Fuck you, CA! You take everything. Fuck you! Fuck you! Fuck yooooooooou!' I beat my fists into the cushions and howled.

My eyesight started to deteriorate as time went on. During 2017 and 2018, reading was becoming difficult. My professor suggested a device that makes reading easier. It cost one hundred and sixty dollars. I told him I didn't have that sort of money to spare, but maybe later, if I was in a better position financially, I could buy one. The next time I saw my professor, he handed me the device. I told him I couldn't take it as I couldn't pay for it.

"It's a gift," he said.

It was a most appreciated gift.

There came the morning that left me feeling humiliated and angry. I was shopping in Woolworths, which I knew very well. I have to know the store well because if I don't, looking up at the signage that tells you what aisle something is in is too hard for me. I get dizzy, and I can't read the signs correctly. I located the aisle I needed. Despite my walking stick, I was very unsteady on my feet, wobbling down the aisle and nearly falling.

"It's only early, and you shouldn't be drinking to the point of being intoxicated. At your young age, it's disgusting."

He was an older man. The look on his face said it all. I felt sick and faint.

I needed to hold on to something. A young man who worked in the store was on his knees stacking shelves, and I made it over to him and grabbed his head. The poor young guy didn't know what was happening, and for a while, I couldn't speak. He realised, however, that I was ill, and he stayed with me until I could communicate what was happening. I clung to him. He assured me that everything was going to be all right. All I wanted to do was leave. People were staring. A neighbour arrived to pick me up. Later, I would try again with more sleep and more medication.

Try again, I told myself.

Try again.

14. Bucket List

Sometime after that, I was walking up the road to the fruit and vegetable shop not far from where I live. I had been to a yoga class that morning, and although I was exhausted, I felt I still had the energy to walk up the hill. On the way back home, I had my walking stick in one hand and two bags of groceries in the other. I was so wobbly on my feet that I ended up walking on the road instead of the footpath. The bags, which were not heavy, now felt so heavy that I feared I might drop them. I repeated to myself, *Just down the hill, and you're almost home. You can do it.*

A car pulled up next to me.

"Good morning; you seem to be having trouble staying on the footpath. We'd just like to know if you're all right?"

"I'm not drunk," I told them. "I have a brain disease."

"Have you consumed any alcohol or drugs?"

"No," I told them. "I have a brain disease."

The police officers looked at me, and I saw a flicker of concern cross their faces.

"Didn't you hear the cars honking at you? You came very close to being hit. You were all over the road. You're still on the road. Can you get onto the footpath, please?"

"Yes, I can. I'm sorry, but like I said, I have a brain disease."

I moved onto the footpath. The officers pulled their car into the kerb and got out. I told them I could hear cars honking, but I thought drivers were impatient with other drivers and didn't associate the noise with me. The officers asked me where I lived, and I gave them my address.

"Would you mind if we took you home? It would make us feel a lot better knowing you are off the road and safe at home."

I nodded, and then it hit me that I had made no distinction between the road and the footpath. So intent on getting home, I had just focused on that goal without thinking about how I was getting there. One officer took my shopping bags, and the other took my arm to steady me, and we walked to my house. They asked if they could come in and see me settled. I gave them the keys. One put my shopping on the table while the other helped me sit on the lounge. We exchanged names, and they told me to rest and that they would let themselves out.

"Take care, Melissa, and please, we never want to see you in the middle of the road again."

I appreciated their help and compassion, and later, I smiled to myself when I thought about being questioned about consuming drugs. I could have given them a list twenty pages long – all legal, of course.

Something else happens when you've lived a lot of your life in a suit and power heels and then find yourself with a walking stick, hair pulled back, flat shoes and sensible clothes. I had become invisible to men. I knew it had been happening for some time, and although it might sound shallow, for me, it was devastating. I tried to ignore it for as long as possible until I had to face the truth – men would no longer look at me like they did before. It was a hard pill to swallow. I had always been able to attract men. I was aware of the effect I had on them. I was attractive, slim, healthy, and worked out at the gym. Sometimes, I'd notice men looking at me, and it did a lot for my self-esteem. Now, I want to be invisible. A close friend tells me that many people with disabilities can form relationships. She says never say never. I know that other people with disabilities have met partners, but I don't feel that I will ever have a relationship again.

There are times when I become very self-conscious. Shopping centres are difficult. People are aware of me. They move out of the way when they see me coming. They tell their children to move and to be careful. It's done out of consideration, and for that, I'm thankful, but it doesn't lessen the loss I feel when I see others shopping and wish I could walk down the aisles just like them. When I see and overhear suited-up people on their mobile phones brokering deals and talking in the business language that I once used, I feel a stab to the heart. I ache for my old life, where I was in charge, making substantial business deals and carrying responsibility for well-known companies. I have had to let it go, and I'm still working on that. I know that I have been in denial at times, pretending that I could still work when I couldn't, but I was only trying to protect myself from any more bad news. I've had to say goodbye to the career I loved, and it was a bitter parting.

The tremors that I had been experiencing were becoming worse and were now becoming seizures. Epilepsy drugs were the answer to this. Before going onto the epilepsy drugs, I had developed a method for controlling the fits. If a leg behaved uncontrollably, I'd sit on the floor with that leg under me to stop shaking. If it was an arm, I'd do the same by lying on the floor and putting my weight on it. As time went by, the method wasn't working well, with an added problem of not getting up off the floor. Even though I didn't want to be on epilepsy medication, it has helped with the fitting. I also realised I could no longer bend down because I'd fall flat on my face as soon as I leaned forward. If I have to pick up something I've dropped, I must first ease myself onto the floor, then strategically have a method to get myself up again. I've developed a technique that uses eight moves, carefully holding onto furniture and moving each arm and leg in a specific pattern. I'm sure I'm exercising my brain at the same time by having to work it all out!

I also developed strategies when walking my dog. I must have a jacket with pockets for my keys and any other items I need because I have a walking stick in one hand and the dog on the lead in the other. He chooses which path he wants to take, as there are several paths around where I live. I've taught him that he can only go off lead in side streets and lanes. He starts to pull when we get to these places, so I let him off immediately. If I don't, he could easily pull me over. I can't handle him pulling me and trying to stay upright with the walking stick simultaneously. He has learnt hand signals, and he generally obeys them. He's a Spoodle, and they are very smart dogs. He watches my hands and takes his cue from them. After we get home, and if he has obeyed his instructions on the walk, he dances around because he knows he's about to get a treat. I can't ever take an untrained dog for a walk, especially a large dog, as I would end up in the gutter. When I was in rehab, my friend minded him for a while. One morning, I got a text, and there was a beautiful picture of my dog with the caption, 'Morning, Mum.' It honestly filled my heart with joy. Sometimes, I can't walk him, so a walker takes over when I can't.

Recently, I've had my bathroom modified so that I can move around and do what I need to do without falling. A bath requires using four different rails.

I have to hang on to a rail with one hand and dry myself with the other when I've finished bathing. I have the things I need in front of me because I have to be very steady if I turn my head or body around. As for swimming, I'm not allowed to do that by myself anymore. I can't cut my toenails anymore as I fall over. I've tried sitting down to do it, but it's still too hard to bend or lift a leg. As for shaving and waxing, forget it. When I attempt to shave my legs and bikini line, I end up cutting myself.

I was on track for a bowel operation, but I needed to put on some weight. I'd become painfully thin, and my doctors wanted me to address this. I was put on a program for people with eating disorders. This program looked at my relationship with food and how it was related to my emotions. I found it hard to follow the program at times because it required total honesty. I had to record everything I ate. This was a program where I was asked some questions about food intake and routine, plus reporting on my emotional state. It tracks behaviour around food. It makes people more aware of what and when they eat and how it is tied to what's going on emotionally. The doctors told me to eat whatever I wanted. It was important to get some food into me. Gradually, I put on a bit of weight. My friends said I looked better. I was gearing myself up for the operation, but physically, I was falling apart.

"Just a fall," I'd say when someone commented on a new bruise or a wobbly gait. The problem was that the falls were happening more often. A few months later, my specialist sat across from me and looked at me with a serious look on his face. He spoke gently.

"You need to start doing some of the things on your bucket list," he said. "All right," I replied.

I didn't cry. I wasn't afraid. However, when I had to fill in an advanced care plan, the reality set in. There it was, on paper. The documentation that put in place those areas that would mean the beginning of the end. The one thing that concerned me was Ughboot. My friend Jack had promised my dog he would go to him when the end came. I made a will and had to start thinking about a guardianship.

I wasn't in denial. My specialist was honest with me, and I appreciated this. I had been struggling all year with physical tasks, and they had gradually become worse. Then came a restricted driving licence, which limited me to thirty kilometres. Driving itself wasn't difficult; the problem was with my eyesight. When I was in my car and about to pull out from the curb, I often couldn't tell whether a car was parked or whether it was moving. It was the problem I experienced some years ago, but now I knew its origin. I developed a method that helped; I'd close one eye. As soon as one eye was closed, I could see whether a car was moving or stationary. Sometimes, when I was driving, I closed one eye because if I didn't, I'd see three cars where there was only one. I often took the longer route if I knew where the traffic lights were, as I didn't have to turn my head too fast. It took longer, but it was the safer option.

I started the bucket list with a visit to Costco with a friend. I'd never been. The staff gave me a scooter, and before long, I was whizzing around Costco, laughing and having fun. By the end of the visit, I had terrible nausea because I was moving my head from side to side, looking at all the merchandise. We went early, which was good as no one was there, so I had all the aisles to myself to ride around as fast or slow as I wanted. I was surprised by how fast the scooter went, but the speed appealed to me. I had to slow down as everything was becoming a blur.

Some months ago, I was in a café. I didn't realise how my hands were shaking, and I dropped the coffee cup, sending shards of ceramic and lots of coffee all over the floor. Lately, I've had a problem with loss of feeling when it comes to hot and cold. I've burnt myself because I've picked up something hot, but I held it for too long as I couldn't feel it was hot. It's the same with cold. Now, if I want to take a cup of tea to bed, I have to use a plastic cup to feel the sensation of heat a bit better and only fill it halfway.

Over the past few months, new changes have happened. I must always walk with my head down, concentrating on the footpath or the grass. A small crack or uneven surface, a rock, a stick, or anything irregular can cause a fall. Simple things began to be a challenge. Buttons on clothes and shoelaces were starting to be too difficult to cope with, so they became shoes without laces and clothes that didn't have buttons. Putting clothes on is a matter of sitting down and deciding what clothes are easiest to get into and don't require that much energy being put into that task. Inserting tampons is ridiculously hard. I often feel unbalanced and fall over, so everything has to be thought out before performing a physical task, where I will place my legs, feet, arms, and hands, is crucial as it means the difference between falling and not falling. That little compressed cotton bullet has a lot of power when you've got CA!

Washing and styling hair is so complicated that it happens with far less frequency than it used to. Many people who can't perform this task take to wearing beanies and hats like I do at times. Now, the hairdresser has to wash it and dry it.

One of the most frustrating things about my body breaking down is the deterioration of speech. I have started to slur my words. I have to make all my phone calls in the morning because the slurring is quite bad in the afternoon and at night, and people won't understand what I'm saying. I sound like I've just had two bottles of Vodka. Before I make a phone call, I do my speech pathology exercises to help with the physical movements of my mouth.

My sleep patterns are becoming worse, and now I need sleeping pills. Even with their help, my sleep is still fractured. I now need to sleep for at least an hour during the day. At night, when I lie still, I can feel the pain inside. The headaches are there all the time. The migraines have lessened. Fifteen migraines a month have now been reduced to four. This is because of the sixty Botox injections that I am having into my head. I walk out of there looking like a bloodied mess. Even though I have tissues to wipe away the blood, it still runs from the scalp down my face. The first time I had it, I felt the irony of that conversation I overheard between my mother and sister. Yes, I probably am the first one in my family to have Botox, but little would they guess it's because my brain is shrinking, and I have incurable migraines. The first time I had to have Botox, my friend told me that I'd better go to the bathroom and clean myself up because I was scaring the other patients. One patient stopped me one morning and said, "Oh, you've had Botox!"

It's good to know that other people understand and look just as scary as me! Eating is painful because it hurts when the top and bottom teeth meet. Soft food is better than hard. Brushing my teeth is also painful because I often stab the insides of my cheeks as I become more uncoordinated. The neurosurgeon explained that the nerve endings in the teeth are breaking down. Now, when I can get out to a café, I have to ask that the crusts be cut off the bread as they are too hard to eat and eating around them is too hard. The lovely owner of my local café suggested I have my favourite toppings on a soft milk bun. It was an excellent suggestion. Many people are so understanding, which is fantastic.

The physical signs of deterioration can't be ignored. I know what they mean.

"You're winning," I said to Cerebral Atrophy, "But I'm not done yet, and you won't be interfering with my bucket list. It's mine, not yours, and I'm going to do it."

Over the following weeks, I started a list. The list included big things that I wanted to do. It also included smaller things like going to Cosco because I'd never been there. I had always wanted to go to Canberra to see Floriade. I wanted to go to Dreamworld, see the baby tigers, and swim with the dolphins. I had swum with them once before and wanted to do it again. I would love to play Paintball and go bike riding if those activities are possible. I wanted my home repainted and decorated. A friend said he could put shutters on the windows for me as I've always liked their look. I'd also like to have the carpet ripped up and have the floorboards polished. I started to plan the things I wanted to achieve.

There would be an interruption to those things with the impending bowel operation. I needed to build up my body before they operated. I was only forty-five kilos and needed to put on some weight. I knew I would have to have a colostomy bag for six to eight months, and I prepared myself for this as well, even though I didn't want it. There were a few weeks of anxiety and stress before this operation because I knew there was a chance that I would not make it. I was prepared for this, but it was very daunting, nevertheless. I worked on my diet and my mental preparation, and finally, the morning arrived. I had confirmed everything the Friday afternoon before as my operation was booked for Monday. It was afternoon surgery. I could have my last meal on Sunday before midday and then clear fluids after that, but I could drink water till 11.00 am on Monday. I followed the fasting rules.

I arrived at the hospital at noon. I presented myself and was told to take a seat. My friend could only stay with me till 2.15 pm as he had parked on Parramatta Road, which became a clearway from 3 pm. I spent four hours in pre-admission. There, I met the team who would operate on me. They wanted to take me through the procedure to make sure I had a better understanding of what would happen.

Three and a half magazines later and some sport watching as well, I was called in and labelled with my ID bracelets. Then, there were the questions every patient must answer before an operation. Height, weight, last time I ate, drank, did I have any crowns, dentures, any metal objects in my body, did I smoke, drink, take drugs and was allergic to anything? My professor advised that I was running two hours late due to complications with another patient, and was sent back to the waiting room to wait until called.

I had a terrible migraine; I was given two Panadeine Forte. At 2.15 pm, my friend left to rescue his car. He asked me to send him a text with a star so he would know everything was going ahead. I was moved to another waiting room where I could rest, and the staff turned off all the overhead lighting. I was only there for ten minutes when a nurse appeared and called my name. After such a long wait, I once again prepared myself mentally.

I was directed to change, put on the pressure stockings, the gown that does up at the back, the attractive (not!) paper undies and blue paper socks. A blood pressure cuff was attached, chest stickers and monitors were connected, and equipment that assists with my brainwaves and sedation was attached to my forehead. I was ready to go. The anaesthetist put in a cannula. I was looking at the clock. She was having trouble with the cannula. She told me that because patients have to fast, finding a vein is more difficult.

It was a quarter to four. A nurse was on the phone, trying to locate another nurse to replace her as she was meant to finish at three-thirty pm. My hand was bleeding due to the size of the cannula, but there was no one there to assist me. At four-thirty, the surgeon appeared and looked through my file. We discussed a few medical decisions, and he returned to the theatre, but not before saying, "I'll see you in a minute. The anaesthetist swill be straight out to do a little something." I thought about drifting into sleep very soon, and the migraine would disappear. The pain of the last few months and the intense pain medication would be gone. I waited and waited, and at five o'clock, the surgeon came through the door. He told me he had some bad news; he would have to put in a stoma bag. I didn't care. I just wanted it over. "That's OK", I told him.

"That's not the bad news," he informed me. "We can't operate", he said. "This theatre has to close by six, and your procedure will take two-and-a-half to perhaps even seven hours."

"So what? You put me upstairs and operate first thing tomorrow. Well, that's very disappointing, but OK."

"No, you go home, and we reschedule."

He also informed me that he was booked out for months.

I couldn't believe it. I had fully prepared myself for being sliced open and having the procedures done that the staff had carefully explained to me. But on top of all that, I had prepared myself for death. Only weeks before, I had gotten my affairs in order. Now, I had to go through all that mental preparation again. I felt numb.

"Again, I am so sorry," the surgeon said. "Call my secretary, and we will work something out", he told me. And with that, he was gone.

A team of nurses came straight out to remove everything they had previously put in. They did it so quickly that it was like I was being prodded at from all different directions. I lay there in silence. Nothing felt real. Nothing made sense. The anaesthetist came out, removed the enormous cannula, and cleaned my hand. He offered to take me back to the previous room. I could tell everyone was sorry and felt for me, but that didn't make it any easier. The nurses had already arranged for all my belongings to be brought to me. I just wanted to change and get out of there before they saw the tears.

I called Jack. He was surprised to hear my voice but came straight away. I was too upset to talk, and he understood. I wasn't sure I believed the theatres had to be closed by six. I suspected that everyone just wanted to go home after a long day.

Despite living with an illness that's going to kill me, there are still some moments where humour can make my day. I read a story about a woman in Adelaide desperately seeking a bone marrow donor. I've already got the donor thing covered in my will if they can use any part of me. I wanted to help the woman in Adelaide, so I told my doctor about the woman and asked her if I could donate to this woman.

"Your bone marrow sucks," my doctor said.

"Ok," I said, and then we both looked at each other and burst out laughing.

Not long after that visit, there came the day when my independence was curtailed forever.

I was driving to the dog groomer in Glebe and was coming out of a side street when my spatial perception was not doing what it should. I mounted the gutter and hit a pole. I didn't have time to be in shock because I was worried about Ughboot sitting in the front seat. The police came straight away. Since the accident happened opposite a café, I assume someone had rung them. I had to ring the pet shop to cancel Ughboot's grooming.

I wasn't charged. I told the police what had happened. They saw that I had a disability sticker. They were really lovely. They got Ugh out of the car, and they didn't say anything about him not being strapped in. They asked me if I was alright, and they drove me home, and I organised a tow truck. I was so intent on arranging the tow truck and making sure Ughboot was all right that I suppressed what might be coming next. A visit to my doctor confirmed the worst.

"You can't drive anymore," she said.

The car was written off. I took the number plates back to the RTA and dealt with the insurance. I didn't fully process what was happening even though I sat down and made a list of the pros and cons of not having a car. I'd save money. I couldn't go out when I wanted to. I'd have subsidised transport. Parking at the hospital would no longer be a problem; it was often difficult to get a park, even with a disability sticker. I could no longer do Mystery Shopping. Mystery Shopping at least brought in a little bit of money. When I first started doing it, I experienced the bitter irony of now doing it when, in my other life, I used to organise marketing people to do it and report back to me.

The loss of my independence was more significant than all of that, however, and it hit me hard.

"You low-life bastard! I hope you're happy!" Cerebral Atrophy did not reply.

Some mornings, I'd wake up and think, 'I'll go to Woolworths today', and then realise that I couldn't just get in my car and go when I wanted to. The car was my lifeline to the world outside the home, and now the car was no more, and I knew I had to adjust to new ways of getting around. Jack said he'd do the food shopping for me, which I appreciated, but food shopping got me out of the house, and I would miss it. Jumping in the car gave me a feeling of intense independence. I was now stuck within the walls of the house. Another issue with others offering to take me places, as grateful as I am, is the loss of privacy. Everybody knows where you want to go and what you buy. Not long ago, a friend offered to take me to a book fair, but he forgot he had made plans with me, so on the day, I didn't go. I wasn't annoyed. It was a kind offer; it was his car and his time, and he had a lot on at the time, so I didn't say anything.

I have quite a few accidents these days. A while ago, I got out of a taxi near my front gate after returning from rehab. I steadied myself against the taxi and had my walking stick out when the taxi suddenly pulled away. Down I went into the gutter. The fall took all the energy out of me. There was no one around. I couldn't stand up, so I crawled on my hands and knees, with my walking stick and my bag, to my front gate. Once there, I could hang on to the gate and pull myself up. The only upside to these episodes is that they teach you to think outside the square, especially if no one can help. At first, falling like this was frightening. I tended to panic. Now, I'm very calm. I lie there and think, surveying my surroundings.

Questions and possibilities run through my head.

OK. If I roll slightly to the left, I can hang on to that pole and hoist myself up. Can I reach my mobile with my other arm?

Will that person across the road see me?

Have I got enough energy to pull myself up, holding onto this window ledge?

It's the same when I walk Ughboot on the days I can. If he wants to go a certain way, I have to consider if it is wise to go that way. He is very determined. And so, the questions begin: *Can I make it all the way up that slope today?*

With hills and slopes, it is a matter of trying not to stop. When going uphill, if I fall, I fall backwards. When going downhill, I fall forward. Even simple surroundings are an obstacle course.

How a bus pulls in is an issue. Some bus drivers take off before people have seated themselves. This is bad enough for a non-disabled person, but for people with disabilities, there is always the fear that the driver will take off before they're seated. Then they'll find themselves on the bus floor or colliding with another passenger or both. Getting off the bus is the same, and having to tap off is an absolute pain as it's one more physical move that we have to think about while trying to steady ourselves, manoeuvre a walking stick, hold onto a bag or parcel and step off without falling. Sometimes, when I'm getting off the bus, my eyes fail me, and it is difficult to know how many steps down are in front of me. Occasionally I see double the amount of steps, even though I know that's not possible. At times I see the steps at a strange angle, off to the right slightly. Again, I know this is not real, but it adds an extra layer of anxiety when alighting from the bus. My heart beats very quickly when I have to get off a bus.

By this time, I'm sweating all over just from the stress of it all.

At times I think people are staring and wishing I would just get off quickly; they probably aren't, but it makes me feel self-conscious. It got to the stage where I could no longer do public transport. If I fall, I have taught myself to laugh. It the best medicine, and I just start all over again. I've learnt to integrate falls into my life. It's strange what you get used to.

Fall. Laugh. Fall.

Laugh.

Rinse and repeat.

15. Teapot and Sympathy

Over the months, the loss of my car has affected me badly. I now walk to the shops if I can, but this means that the effort I have to exert is so taxing that I need a rest before I walk to the shops and then a sleep when I get home. The mental effort is tiring as well as it requires great concentration to negotiate the path, sticks, stones, and anything else that can cause a fall. I have to scan my surroundings and ask some questions: Is the concrete even? Is that a fallen berry over there? Oh no, there's a crack. I'll have to be careful there.

Shit. A carton right in the middle of the footpath. How will I get around this group of people in the middle of the footpath if they don't move?

My professor recently asked me if I'd like to help train doctors and young medical students who were thinking about going into an area that specialises in diseases like mine. I told him I'd be happy to help.

I'd developed such a good relationship with him that I now called him a nickname when I suspected he was holding back information about how the next phase of deterioration would affect me. Because his name has connotations with the process of making tea or coffee, I came to call him 'Teapot.'

When he explained why specific actions were becoming hard for me, I'd say, 'Well, that's just great, Teapot,' or 'Come on, Teapot! Can't you do something?'

Occasionally I'd hear about people with other diseases with symptoms similar to mine being helped by new drugs.

'Can't I have that new drug too, Teapot? Wouldn't it help me if the symptoms are the same?'

He explained that although the symptoms might be similar, those drugs wouldn't help me. It was frustrating to hear this, but at least he was honest with me. On the morning I was helping out the trainees, he explained that they would like to ask me questions. I told him I was happy to answer any questions – even if they were questions about delicate areas.

'Good,' said my professor. 'But don't call me 'Teapot' in front of them.'

I started to laugh, and so did he. I liked joking around with him, and I often made him laugh.

The trainees were great. First of all, they had to observe me and try to guess what disease I had. Some of them came very close. Because my symptoms are similar to Multiple Sclerosis, most people assume I have MS. Sometimes, when people ask me what my condition is, I often say it's MS, only because I haven't got the energy to explain about Cerebral Atrophy. MS is a much more publicised condition, and many people know something about it. The students asked me lots of questions, and I was happy to be able to help them better understand the disease. I loved assisting them with learning. I thought to myself: *Well, I'm going to die, so let's have some fun with this training!* Laughter really is the best medicine.

The questions people would like to ask but don't (although some do) are these:

Can you still have sex? Answer: Yes. Degree of difficulty – High. Why? It's nothing to do with the mechanics of the sex act; it's simply to do with tiredness. Does the disease affect a woman's periods? Answer: No. Once again, there is a high degree of difficulty when menstruating. It's easy to tip over when inserting tampons.

Does the disease affect sex drive? Answer: Again, only in terms of tiredness. Do you feel angry that you have this disease? Answer: Yes.

Most people who have this illness and MS and similar diseases have gone through different phases – shock, denial, grief, anger, depression, bargaining, and acceptance, but we don't tend to stay in one phase. Even though I've accepted my disease, my anger flares up when yet another part of my body breaks down. Every new symptom brings a new wave of anger with which I have to deal. I am all right if a new symptom takes a while to manifest itself, but if it jumps ahead and doesn't give me time to adjust and get my head around, then I get angry. Anger and anxiety are not good for me. Cortisol levels rise, energy gets wasted, and then I feel exhausted, so I try to keep a positive spirit as hard as it is.

Is the prognosis accurate about what will happen and when? Answer: Sometimes, but not always. Some of my doctors have been surprised that I have proved them wrong in terms of the length of time that I have carried on without certain things happening.

Are you scared of losing your mental faculties? Answer: Absolutely terrified. But I'm doing everything I can to keep my brain alive.

I was pleased to be able to give the trainee medical students an insight into the physical and mental difficulties that those with diseases like mine have to contend with, and I was happy to help out my professor. Recently, I thought I might like to get a small tattoo on the back of my neck, so I asked him about it.

'No,' said Teapot. 'It's too near the part of the neck. It's close to where things are connected to the cerebellum.'

'You sound like my Dad when you say no,' I told him.

'Perhaps you need fatherly advice as well as professional advice as well,' he said and laughed. 'No tattoo. That's the end of this discussion.'

The Botox doctor said no, as well. If I needed a cortisone injection into that area, then it might cause problems. I sighed and accepted the answer. They run my life now, but I know what they do is right for me.

I was still working with my psychologist. We were making small breakthroughs in my journey to feel good about myself. I knew that I had suppressed a lot of emotions, particularly at the time when I was first diagnosed, but I kept on working.

"I'd put on my mask," I told her.

I realised that I hadn't just been putting on a mask to delay the knowledge of what was going to happen to my body. I'd been putting on a mask all of my life. I'd put it on when my mother said horrible and untrue things about me.

"Why did you put on that mask when she said those things?"

I realised that I was so desperate for her approval that I'd put on a happy face even when I was hurting so badly, I'd go and cut myself. Everything I did was to gain her approval of me. I never stopped trying for years. I'd do the same with work; I'd be falling apart, but my mask would go on, and no one would know the difference. James had shown me no compassion when I was assaulted, and yet I pushed it down and masked up and went on with my marriage. The mask was part of the walls I had been putting up for years. I'd go back in my mind to my bedroom when I was a child. The space where I was safe and quiet, and the outside world could not come in.

Through working with a psychologist, I came to see that I behaved the way others wanted me to behave. I learned that wearing a mask is not committing to your true self or genuine emotions. Masking blocks your real thoughts. After a while, you don't know who you really are because you've never experienced autonomy to be yourself and make decisions based on what's right and true. I was a people pleaser. I realised that letting go of that mask would not be easy. I'd started to see the masked Melissa as the real me. I'd accepted it as me, sometimes pushing the real me down into non-existence. I didn't know how to function without it. I'd lost sight of who I was and what I needed. I'd been conditioned by my mother to think of myself as worthless. I'd climbed to the top of my career, masking at times, and when that ended, I had to re-think my whole life. I'd look in the mirror, and the person reflected at me was someone I'd made up.

It made me reassess my work ethic as well. I'd become ambitious in my climb to the top. I was hard on myself and hard on others. This hardness came from my will to survive. I'd survived childhood cruelty, but I'd taken that hardness into my working life. I felt no compassion when I had to sack someone. I didn't stop to think about how this would affect their life, health and finances. I couldn't. I was surviving myself and had nothing left to give others.

Masking allows you to be brave. It enables you to feel powerful because you have control of the situation. After all, no one is touching the real you, and no one has control but you. You think this, but it is not true. People pleasing is exhausting, and in the end, those people have power over you. I needed to take back control of my life. And the hard thing was that I had to take back control of my life at a time when everything in my life was in a state of no control.

I put on my mask for James as well, but as the years go by, I find I have anger towards him. Since I've been analysing my life and working with a psychologist, I often now wonder why he married me in the first place. Did marrying me make him a better man? Did he think he could get to the top of his career like I had done by being with me? I look back at James now, and I see he was a very weak person. I am at fault as well. I set a snare for him to fall into, and he fell into it. This should have been a red flag for me, but I was young and naive and believed in the fairy tales of 'the one', 'the marriage', 'the kids' and 'happily ever after'. The older and wiser person I've become would advise against the type of behaviour

I indulged in, but I have to forgive myself for that, too. I didn't know any better, and I was raised in a dysfunctional household. As I become older, I realise that we are all mostly brought up to believe in dreams, the dream of falling in love, getting married, having children, having a great career and being healthy and happy. We know that illness and divorce happen, but we don't expect it to happen *to us*. I had to admit that I had spent a lot of my life living my mother's dreams, not mine. I was kept from making my own choices because of *her* needs. I have to let go of the past. I have to say goodbye to the marriage and that part of my life.

Another aspect I have come to terms with is seeing my life as a series of choices I made that had consequences but not thinking about them as 'mistakes.' I have come to see them as lessons in life. Some of them may not have been the best choices, but what is important is what I have learned from them. If I had kept repeating the same behaviour and choices, then I could have called them 'mistakes', but since I have not repeated my choices in the last few years, I have come to see them differently.

As time has gone by, I have begun to understand how desperately I had needed my mother's approval. My brothers and sisters seemed to receive it automatically from my mother, whereas I always had to work hard for it. She was embarrassed, ashamed and annoyed by me. I had always been 'worthless', 'useless', 'annoying', had a 'bad attitude', 'no logic' and 'would never become anything'. The worst part was my brothers and sisters also got in on the act. And they got in on the act because they were encouraged to do so and had my mother as the role model for putting me down.

I kept on with therapy, and one afternoon, there was a breakthrough that even I didn't see coming. As hard as it was, I had made progress in not hating myself and blaming myself for everything that had happened. I now understand that my upbringing had been abusive. I now understood that the attention-seeking that I was accused of was because the attention was drawn away from my mother. She developed a behaviour that drew the attention back towards her by using me as her long-suffering burden. The more time I spent in therapy, the more I realised just how cruel my mother had been to me. It took a long, long time to get my head around it. How could someone give birth to a child and hate it so much?

While I was in therapy, I came across a story about a girl whose mother was diagnosed with Munchausen Syndrome by Proxy. Munchausen by Proxy is a syndrome where the caretaker of a child either makes up fake symptoms or causes real symptoms to make it appear as though the child is injured or ill. I was genuinely ill; my mother didn't cause my illness, so that label can't be given to her. However, further research led me to read about another form of MSP in which the caregiver causes psychiatric or psychological damage to the child to make them unstable by telling them they are mentally unwell or crazy or a nutcase. I felt the hairs on my arms rise up. I was sweaty. I couldn't stop reading. I felt like I was reading about me. I had to stop reading at times because I was overcome with emotion. It was a light bulb moment. It was as though I had been seeing everything through a haze and now the fog had lifted, and everything was clear.

A mother who wanted her daughter to be mentally unstable so the mother could have all the attention. A mother who told her daughter that she was a nutcase, so much so that her daughter ended up with a severe psychiatric condition. I felt like I was reading about my own life. Many of the elements of this phenomenon were exactly like my mother's. My mother would love to regale all the procedures I was having, the medications, the visits to doctors, specialists and surgeons, the time it took, and the stress it put her under. She had no qualms about my privacy. The role of the patient, the sick one, was a role that she was denied when she was a child. When I got sick, she was resentful that I got the help that I needed. She turned that resentfulness into a cry for attention for herself by playing the role of the long-suffering mother. She told me from a young age that I was a 'nutcase', a 'fruit-loop', 'useless', that I'd always be 'sick' and 'dependent' on her.

One morning, my psychologist and I were delving into my mother's hatred of me, her adoration of James, her flirtatious behaviour around him, her need to see him even though we were divorced and her constant attempts to keep in contact with him until his new wife stopped it. We had been discussing this for months, teasing out various elements of my mother's motivations.

'Why do you think she behaved that way where James was concerned?'

'Because she was in love with him.'

Did I just say that? Shit. What have I just said? The words were finally out. And with them came a long-ago suppressed memory, a conversation with my sister. My sister had said: *If Mum could have sex with James, she would.* It made me feel sick. But it all made sense. I sat back, shocked by the revelation. Somewhere, I had suppressed what I'd suspected. It was too awful to contemplate, so I'd stowed it away and pretended it didn't exist. Once the words were out, I felt something shift. It was as though the earth had just tilted swiftly in one direction and then quickly righted itself. I felt it in my body, a profound, visceral truth. It was revolting and completely liberating at the same time. This wasn't just her cruelty.

'My own mother was *jealous* of me.'

More was coming out. My psychologist just nodded quietly. I could tell it was one of those moments where she had been waiting for this realisation to emerge. Another light bulb moment. At last. Over the next few months, I began to understand that my mother had poisoned the whole family against me because she was jealous. It was an excruciating process. My sisters were raised to be jealous of me, and my father and brother saw me as a problem to be solved. I was the loser, the one who wouldn't amount to anything, and when I did climb my way to the top, they gave credit to my ex-husband as if I couldn't have done the same thing as a single person. I also think that my sisters were attracted to James in some respects as well, not in the way my mother was but more in a general way.

I came to understand that my affair was just as much about me not deserving happiness as a need to rebel as well. All my life, I had been controlled. My mother had me under her thumb. I had to do everything the doctors told me to do. Then, I put James' needs above my own and let him control the marriage. I'd never been free to make decisions on my own. The affair was about me desperately trying to find a space of my own. My husband had never been supportive and had come to side with my mother, and I'd become used to thinking that I deserved to be punished. I felt I was useless because I couldn't give him children, and that's what he wanted. My mother was so jealous of me that the sicker I became, the worse her treatment of me because I was getting all of the attention and attention was deflected away *from her*. I would give anything not to have all of the attention I need from the medical profession, and I can't understand anyone not becoming more compassionate as their child gets sicker.

My mother was hospitalised many times as a child. She never got any attention from her own dysfunctional, alcoholic parents. Her parents were completely emotionally unavailable, and because of this, I believe she came to think that 'if I had to do it without any support, so can Melissa.' I never found out why she was in hospital so many times, but perhaps she, like me, was in pain because of her coeliac disease and was never treated properly. I know that because of her upbringing, she was a survivor. However, the experience of her younger days damaged her, and all that damage culminated in her resentment of me. When her 'parents,' who were, in reality, her aunt and uncle, passed away, her ill-treatment of me increased.

She was resentful of me because of the treatment I was receiving, and so became the martyr. She turned my sisters against me because I was the pretty one with a slim figure and clear skin, attributes neither of them had. She was jealous that James was attracted to me, and she fuelled that jealousy in my sisters. To get the attention she craved, she told lies and manipulated people into behaving how she wanted them to. Her self-esteem was probably very low. She didn't know how to mother anybody, and she had quite an attractive and ill daughter. That daughter took up a lot of her time and got the medical attention she required. I believe she resented the fact that nobody had supported and comforted her when she was growing up. Then, when that daughter met a very attractive man, the resentment increased to the point where she was determined to wreck the marriage. I know now that I married James because of her. I married him because I believed I would be loved. Years of brainwashing her other children meant that they only saw events through her eyes. Working with my psychologist, I can now see what she did to get that attention.

Both my sisters had problems in their marriages. There were many fights, which were often caused by some seed that my mother had planted in one or another of the couples' heads. Then, her daughters would come running to her for help and advice. She would then sweep in like a superhero and 'fix' the problem. This made them dependent on her. They just couldn't see how she operated. They were too close to her. In the same way, my relationship with her was built on a sick co-dependency. I thought of her as my best friend.

Her other method of getting attention was to play the martyr. "Look at me, everybody! Sacrificing myself for my sick child!" Her friends fawned all over her, giving her sympathy and consolation for her terrible lot in life. My mother wanted me to deteriorate. She didn't like the fact that I fought against my illness. There are many parents out there who have children with disabilities, children with terminal diseases, psychiatric conditions, psychological problems, and other issues. Their parents still love and nurture them and would do anything to make their child's life more comfortable.

My psychiatrist and my psychologist both believe that it is plausible that my mother had some psychiatric form of Munchausen by Proxy of the psychiatric type – she wanted her daughter to be ill and not just ill – mentally ill. I will never know because it is my decision never to see her again. There's nobody left to ask on her side regarding her mental health, as they've all passed away. I've done enough reading to know that she possibly has Borderline Personality Disorder. Because this is a disorder of personality, it isn't easy to treat. I see now that my mother had me so attached to her that I believed only she could save me. I would leave home in the morning, say goodbye at the door, and call her as soon as I got to work.

I was totally enmeshed with her. Now I know that the relationship between mother and daughter was an unhealthy and dangerous one. I've read up about Stockholm Syndrome, the psychological state where hostages or abused people bond with their abusers over some time. The victim identifies with the abuser, attaches to them, and defends their actions. Friends have asked me why I stayed. Why didn't you leave home as an older teen? Didn't you realise that your family was a bit weird? Didn't you know that your mother's treatment of you wasn't normal? I can only say this: My mother manipulated my thinking from when I was very small. She had me totally enmeshed with her, and I had no other reference to which to compare my family. I didn't discuss my family with friends at school. We were raised to believe that family business was private. And so, I was silent and came to believe that what my mother said was right, that this was the way parents behaved, that this was normal, and that the problem lay with me.

There is something dark and disturbing about my mother. I know her biological parents neglected her, and she developed strategies for survival. I believe, however, that some of those strategies were unhealthy and dangerous.

I wonder about other types of abuse she may have suffered. Was this why she flirted with my ex-husband? Was her self-esteem tied to sexual favours that may have begun as a child? She always craved male attention, and perhaps it explains why. Is this why she interfered with my sisters' marriages and my own – because she couldn't stand to see other people happy and was jealous? She had run the streets until her aunt and uncle took her in and became her parents. Her life had no boundaries, no safety net. What did she have to do to survive? And what lasting damaging legacy did it leave? I will never know. All I know is that it was wrong.

Today, I have a tenuous relationship with my father. Things are gradually improving, but it is a long road back. We have re-established contact after a long period of not speaking to each other. I have come to realise through working with my therapist that my father wasn't that bad. It was my mother who made her children afraid of him. She was the one who put ideas into our heads about pretending to study when our father arrived home; otherwise, he would be angry. She was the one who created fear about our father. Certainly, he was a victim of his own culture and upbringing when it came to how to raise daughters. I believe he is sorry for the way I was raised and the way I was treated, but he can't express his emotions. A Maltese man brought up by a very tough father and a very strong mother, with old-fashioned ideas about women in a men-are-superior world, Dad found it difficult to accept that I was the breadwinner in my marriage. He had problems with accepting that I was the one with the drive and ambition and the one who battled on despite my illness. When I told him that we were scared of him as children, he was quite bewildered. He looked confused and said, 'Really?'

In 2018, my father started experiencing the beginning of dementia. My grandmother had passed away, and, on the evening of the wake, my mother rang my father and told him she was moving out and divorcing him. She moved out that night. I found out later that she had been taking valuables from the house and storing them elsewhere for months, and she'd set up a PO box in a new suburb. I was never shocked at her cruelty to me, but her cruelty to my Dad left me speechless. He was in no position to fight for what was his, and I thought the property settlement was unfair to him when the house was sold. My sister put my mother up to it; she spurred her on, and, in the end, even though I told my Dad I'd help him fight her, my father just wanted it over. My mother decided it was a girls-just-wanna-have-fun time after thirty-five years of marriage. My father deserved much more out of the settlement. There must have been altercations between my father and mother over the divorce and settlement. My father showed me some papers where my mother had signed her name to some untruths. She said that when the children were little, my Dad had insisted that his children call him by his first name and not 'Dad.' This is not true. We always called him 'Dad.' She also said that I had been diagnosed with bipolar. I was outraged when I read that. I felt like going to see her and screaming, 'Who diagnosed me? Name of the psychiatrist? Date? Place? Copy of the paperwork? Factual evidence?'

It just confirmed what I'd read about MSP of the psychiatric branch. She *wants* me to have bipolar. I wouldn't be ashamed if I did have that condition, but I don't, and it is a low act to tell people such a lie.

I believe my father didn't see or didn't want to see my mother's true colours until much later in his life. He was under her thumb as well, and she manipulated him. He was raised in a different culture with different values. It doesn't excuse his not sticking up for me. A few years ago, he took himself on a trip around Australia alone. This would have been unthinkable in the culture he was raised in; it would signify that there were problems in the marriage or that a husband and wife were no longer together. I don't ask much about his relationship with my mother. He knows I never wish to see her again, and he has come to terms with that. When I speak of my mother with my father, I refer to her as 'Satan's mistress.' I will never use the term 'my mother' again. She wasn't a mother.

Before his divorce from her, he'd ring and tell me that he was at Maccas and then ask if I wanted to join him. My first question to him was about *her* or *she* or *ex-wife*. If she was there with him, I didn't go. He told me that the family doesn't have contact with James anymore; his new wife put a stop to it. That's probably the one area the new wife and I would agree on. My mother kept in contact with him for as long as she could before his new wife stopped it. Why would his new partner want him to maintain contact with an ex-mother-in-law? Of course, she would think it strange.

I don't have contact with my sisters. In 2018, one of them rang me. My first thought was that she might have had a change of heart towards me. No. She started berating me about the GoFundMe page I had set up. My medical bills were getting on top of me, and I was struggling financially on my disability pension. My sister was angry because I hadn't said anything about the loving, caring, compassionate sister supporting me. The reason I hadn't posted anything about the loving, caring, compassionate sister who was supporting me was that there was no such sister doing that. She wanted her name in lights. She asked me to amend the webpage and give her some kudos. She then started a rant about the past, and I hung up on her. She hasn't rung since.

Before his divorce, I had lunch with my Dad who handed me fifty dollars. 'It's from your mother,' he said.

'Then you can have it back. I don't want it.'

He told me that my mother and he led separate lives these days.

'Do you still have sex with her?' I asked him. I wasn't voyeuristic. I just needed to know the extent of their 'separate' lives.

'Can we change the subject?' he replied.

Although I was struggling financially, and the money would have been helpful, I didn't want anything from her. If she felt guilty for the way she treated me, then fifty dollars certainly wasn't going to fix it. I never ask about my sister, but my father tells me bits and pieces occasionally. My father and I are going on a cruise together at the end of the year. I'm a bit nervous about it for a few reasons: I don't know how I'll manage if my health packs up on holiday, and I don't know how it will work out spending a week with my Dad, who I'm still getting to know, but I suppose I'll know a lot more after that week. Added to that, I get seasick! People have told me big ships don't rock like small boats, so I hope that's true.

I know now that I have to get to know my father on my own terms. I only ever saw him through my mother's eyes, and her filter on everything is very skewed.

This year has been difficult in terms of the deterioration that I'm experiencing. I try to live in the moment, but it is challenging. Not focusing on the future is hard to do. Every time something happens to another part of the body, it brings up feelings of fear about how bad it will eventually get. It's now 2023, and I'm forty-seven. I don't look my age, and I don't feel it despite my illness. I feel thirty-three. I tell myself every day I'm thirty-three so that the number never change for me. I haven't seen my mother for seventeen years. She has never tried to contact me, and if she did, I'd hang up. In that time, there has been a lot to process. I've had a long journey and have had to make one of the most painful decisions: to cut my toxic family out of my life. I've realised that just because I'm biologically attached to them doesn't mean they are good for me. They say that blood is thicker than water, but as far as I'm concerned, water's done more for me. My friends are there for me. I have wonderful girlfriends and male friends as well. When I feel down, they lift my spirits. Even seeing a friend for half an hour can be a complete mood changer.

I've read many self-help books over the last couple of years. I've concluded that it is not what you read that helps you but *when* you read it. Sometimes, information doesn't resonate because I haven't been ready to accept it, or it hasn't been the right time to read it. I now start every new year reading Jack Hawkins' book *It's Either Now or Too Late*. I've read it many times, but I keep reading it as it reminds me that *happiness is up to me*. Even though there are days when pain and exhaustion overwhelm me, I refuse to give in completely. Another practice that helps me is list writing. When I feel down, I get a piece of paper and make two columns. I write out all the positive things about my life and also negative things. It is pretty easy to fill out the negative column very quickly and much harder to fill out the positive. The point is to find things to put in the positive column. It's not a Pollyanna way of looking at my situation; my situation is terrible, there's no getting past that fact, but I'm forced to find the positive, even in the smallest ways. It makes me grateful for those things.

There are some days when it is tough to be in a positive mood, like three days ago.

I fell from the landing down four thick concrete steps to land face-first at the bottom on the base of the steps, which, unfortunately, is a concrete slab. My face went black and blue, and I cut my eye. It is now day three, and I can see properly. It was challenging to be positive with limited vision, but I have to turn my thoughts around and know that it will heal. On day three, I can laugh about it; day one is a bit early!

I've now got a whole team looking after me. My general practitioner, two neurologists, a psychiatrist, a psychologist, a mental health nurse, a dietician, a gastro-dietician, a bowel specialist, a neuro-ophthalmic specialist, a speech pathologist, two rehab specialists, an occupational health therapist, a personal trainer and a podiatrist and a gynecologist make up the team. I have access to a community shuttle, which takes me to my hospital and rehab visits, and I also have taxi vouchers from the government. My friend Jack calls my team the 'care bears'.

I've lost that business toughness I had in the old days. I've had to admit that I'm not strong and have had to accept that I need a team to help me. I'm so grateful to have these wonderful people who make my life easier.

Although I try to remain positive, there are some days when I still want to end it all, particularly if I'm having a terrible day. Yesterday was one of those. My doctor wrote out all the prescriptions I needed, then asked me if there was anything else I'd like.

"A bullet," I said.

"Oh, yes. A Nutri-bullet. You should get one. Makes very healthy juices."

"No, a bullet. That thing that goes in a gun."

"Can't do that," she said. "Can't write a prescription for that, and the health system wouldn't reimburse you for it."

We looked at each other and burst out laughing.

All my medical therapists and specialists have to be kept in the loop with each other to let the others know what's going on, as a change in medication or a physical change might affect something that the different specialists need to know about. I'm grateful to them all for being honest with me. It's no use sugar-coating the changes that come with this disease. They poke and prod me physically and mentally, but it's all part of monitoring. I'm waiting for some NDIS funding to enable me to go to other therapists, such as acupuncturists, massage therapists, physiotherapists, and speech therapists. I've lost count of the number of neurological tests, laparoscopies, colonoscopies, endoscopies, spinal taps, lumbar punctures, cortisone injections, allergy tests, MRIs, CAT scans and muscle biopsies.

My typical week has changed since I first got diagnosed. On Mondays, I often have to have cortisone injections. Tuesday is an off day. Every Wednesday is rehabilitation. Thursdays are taken up with a visit to my mental health nurse, and sometimes, I have to see my psychiatrist on the same day. The only days I have off are Fridays and the weekends. I used to try and organise everything on the one day, but I can't do that anymore due to energy levels. One thing a day is all I can cope with. I have now taken on Pilates Reformer. It isn't as hard on the body as regular Pilates. I have a class and an instructor to help me. The reformer class is full of people who have arthritis and other afflictions and people like me who don't have the energy for regular classes.

These days, the first thing I see when I open my eyes is the blinds on the windows. If the blinds are moving, I know my brain is not working correctly. There shouldn't be movement. My blinds move often. Soon after that comes nausea. I have to turn away from the blinds until the nausea passes. Then, I begin what is now a typical day. My days used to be very structured, but now it's more about 'going with the flow' because I never know what will happen next.

Everything is done in slow motion. I raise myself from three pillows. I can't sleep flat on my back as my head has to be above my body due to constant nausea. When getting up, I swing my legs over the side of the bed and put one hand on the wall and the other on the bed to stabilise myself. The first few steps I take are still using the bed and the wall. It's usually about ten steps before I'm able to move properly. How well I wake up depends on the quality of sleep I've had the night before. As the disease progresses, sleep patterns become worse. I usually have to knock myself out with medication, and if there is pain anywhere, then heavy drugs like Endone can help.

After I've hoisted myself out of bed, I select what clothes I will wear. Nothing with buttons unless I've got nothing planned for the day. Buttons can take *an hour* to do up. Sometimes, I persist with it. I sit on the floor to put on my clothes; otherwise, I fall easily. Putting on a bra is challenging, and if I have a friend over, I will ask them to help me. Modesty is such a thing of the past! A true friend puts your underwear on for you. Putting on pants is impossible from a standing position as it requires standing on one leg, which just doesn't work. The doctors are talking about putting cortisone injections into my neck as I'm falling quite a bit. I have to make the bed no matter how hard it is. Unless I'm so sick that I know that I'm going to get back into it in a short time, I always make it. Even though it takes a long time, it makes me feel that I've achieved something and am organised. I have to eat breakfast because the medication I take requires food with it. Because eating has become painful, I tried to avoid it for a while, but the weight loss was doing me harm. At the moment, I'm seeing a gastro-dietician, which is great because she gives me ideas about how and what to cook so that eating isn't as painful, and food doesn't become an enemy. I drink my tea from my plastic cup and make sure I can feel the heat. I then take my Ughboot out the back to go to the toilet.

If it's a day where I have to change the sheets, then I won't get a lot done. Changing the sheets is a challenge. If I want to change my sheets, I strip the bed and start washing. After putting on the fitted and flat sheets (more moves than I can count), I have to rest for an hour as the energy expended to do that takes it out of me. I come back after resting and do the pillows and then the doona. If I can get someone to change the doona, I will, as that's the hardest. It takes two stages. *The buttons on the doona cover are a bitch*. It can take up to an hour, but I will persist until they are done. After that, I have to rest again. Washing bed linen and making the bed up can also take place all day, depending on the time I've had short rest periods in between. Sometimes, it's bedtime by the time the bed is made. Everything now is done in slow motion. My friend Jack and I sometimes cook together at my house.

'You're soooooooo slow!' Jack said. 'Next time, you have to start peeling two hours before me.'

He was right. I'm not supposed to use a knife anymore because I'm so uncoordinated, and a plastic knife and a potato don't like each other very much. I'm now buying fruit and vegetables that are already cut up. A friend bought me a dicing machine, and it's great. Eating raw food is good too; not so much cooking, therefore not so much cleaning up.

The physicality of the kitchen is proving a challenge, and I'm making some enquiries about getting some modifications to it. Pulling out drawers and reaching into cupboards doesn't work for me anymore. I need shelves that swing out and cabinets that are the right height.

Dying my hair has become difficult, but I refuse, absolutely refuse, to go grey! I'll get to that point one day – I know people who don't care and couldn't be bothered anymore with covering the grey. It's a small thing, but it makes me feel better. My problem is that the disease won't let colour stay on my hair. The only way to keep the colour in is to use peroxide first. This seems to work. I have a hairdresser who comes to the house. This wonderful man refuses to let me pay him. I am so thankful for the kindness of some people. My physiologist now comes to me because getting to her premises is too difficult. A girlfriend takes me shopping every Monday morning.

I was always quite determined I would never end up in a wheelchair. I have softened my stance and now have a disability scooter. What a liberating thing it is! I still think I should have L plates on it for the safety of others!

Weird things are happening with my eyesight. I was in a café recently, and a woman walked in with a dress with stripes in zig-zag patterns. I couldn't look at it and had to turn my head. I explained to my friend that I wasn't rude, but I couldn't look at that pattern as it made me nauseous. I had to look in another direction while talking to my friend. The same thing happens when I occasionally go to the markets. There is a section with vintage clothes, and sometimes they have terribly busy, loud shirts from the sixties in fluorescent colours and patterns. I avoid that section because seeing those colours and patterns makes me feel like being sick. Brightly coloured yellow often has the same effect. No retro clothes for me!

Television is another area that brings about the same reaction. There are some advertisements that I can't watch. Cars going around and around in circles and stuff like that. Flashing dots and lines, anything that's too busy and fast. Same. When a train pulls into a station, there is that small amount of time before it slows completely. That small amount brings on the effect, as does a bus slowing to a stop.

Washing clothes is an ordeal, but at least I'm getting some exercise. I have to drag the clothes basket down some stairs, one step at a time. The hardest part is putting the washing on the line. I swing on the line to hold myself upright while putting an item on the line. Then, I manoeuvre myself into a position to reach a peg and clip it on. I've had quite a few falls doing this, and my clothesline is now in a U shape because I've dragged it down when I put all my weight in it. After the clothes are dry, I take them back up the steps (much lighter now as they are dry) and start the bed-making process. If I'm going to have a fall, the best place is near a wall because if I fall against a wall, it is easier just to slide down it!

I still do my own housework. Household help is available to people with my condition, but I want to keep doing things for myself for as long as I'm able. I've always been so independent; it's hard to give that up and also to admit that there are certain things that I just can't do anymore. Many people would accept household help, and I understand why, but it is one more thing that I would have to say goodbye to. The ability to still do specific tasks, however slowly, keeps me from having to farewell yet another part of my daily physical routine. At times, when I'm getting stuck into vacuuming, I forget the tiredness. The only way I know I'm tired and have to stop is when I fall over. Sometimes, I trip over the electrical cord. It's the same when cleaning. Sometimes, I trip over nothing at all.

I've decided I am going to shave my head. Washing and drying my hair is beyond me and takes up too much energy. Even though my hairdresser now comes to the house to wash and dry my hair, shaving it will be much easier. I asked him to shave it off last week, and he got upset and told me he couldn't do it. Get somebody else to do that, he told me. It was too much of a reality check for him to acknowledge that I was deteriorating. I understood. At least if I decide to shave it off because of all the Botox into my skull, my bald head will be wrinkle-free forever!

Yesterday, I fell off the bus. I really don't like the new Opal card system. I have a walking stick and a bag; I'm slow and off-balance, which means tapping on and off and trying to remain standing while holding on to something to stay steady while tapping. Other people were trying to tap on and off around me while I fumbled for my card, and then I fell. The old system was much more comfortable as it only required putting the card in once.

People are very kind, and total strangers often help me. I'd rather my friends do practical things for me; that's how to show care. Lately, I've been experiencing ataxia. Ataxia is a loss of muscle control or coordination, affecting limbs, speech, eye movement and swallowing. I was with Jack the first time this happened and knew what would help.

"Quick! Sit on me!" I said.

At first, he seemed bewildered, but once he saw the shaking, he calmly sat on me and stayed there until the ataxia stopped. Then we both laughed our heads off. Now, my friends comply when this rather unusual request comes up. Once, when a friend was sitting on me on the floor, his phone rang. The person on the other end had asked what he was doing.

"Sitting on Melissa," he said. "I'll be a while."

16. The Time of My Life

In 2017, I did one of the things on my bucket list. I went to Floriade. A friend and I went on the bus. When I got there, I hired a mobility scooter and rode around the flower beds. It was so beautiful. I took lots of photos, and I keep looking at the images, the colours of the tulips and my friend and me with big smiles. I don't want to sit around moping. If I can still go out, I will.

If someone comes to pick me up so I don't have to drive, that would be even better. If I know I'm going to have a big day out, then I just take more drugs!

Last week, I asked my professor if I could travel by plane. He sat there for quite some time before he answered. He could see my determination, and I felt he didn't want to squash my enthusiasm for travel.

"Why is your answer taking so long, Teapot?" I asked.

"Because I'm thinking of all the things that could go wrong and how to deal with them at thirty thousand feet," Teapot replied.

Nevertheless, he gave me a letter to take with me if I ever get to fly again. At least I can forget about travel insurance. In the next discussion with him, he suggested that I try flying to somewhere not too far away because if something serious goes wrong, I'm only a short distance from Australia.

In another life, I was earning six figures. Now, every dollar is an issue. I've lived two very different lives. Well-off, a career, a husband, our own home, company cars, overseas holidays, and a family. Now it's the opposite: poor, unemployed and on a disability pension, in public housing, no husband, no overseas holidays and no family. It has been a difficult journey partly because I was so successful in my other life. I had an incredible drive to succeed, but I wouldn't have done so well if I hadn't been very skilled in what I did. How do I succeed in this new, limited life? How do I say goodbye to those days?

While my brain still works, I've been considering ways to bring in extra cash. Mystery shopping is no longer an option now that I don't drive. I've started doing market research. At first, this was hard. Sometimes, I had to catch a bus to the city, then walk. Now, I have to be picky about the research jobs I apply for, as I have to consider the location first. I have done commercials mainly as an extra, which is time-consuming as most take all day. But the upside is I have made some great friends. I still apply for market research jobs because I can't get around very well. I do home scan, where you can scan all your groceries and earn points to spend on items you need. I also do surveys on the computer, mainly for Octopus, as you can redeem money after you reach $20.00 and I also dabble in eBay. If I sell things, the money comes in handy as it pays bills. I know I'm not doing a lot, but I'm still trying.

Despite all the psychological counselling, I'm still working through family stuff, marriage stuff, divorce stuff, disease stuff, depression stuff, and all sorts of stuff. It takes years to process, to see clearly from a distance, and more objectively, why things went so terribly wrong. It has taken me years to get my mother's voice out of my head.

I still have my wedding photos. A close friend suggested I get rid of them. I know that conventional wisdom, Feng Shui and Marie Kondo would tell me that it would be psychologically cleansing to get rid of them. They don't spark joy, but I haven't got to the point of getting rid of them. I don't know how to say goodbye to that time. It was such an enormous chunk of my life. I still struggle with it today.

One of the methods that I have adopted to help me re-frame my thinking is looking at language. It sounds so simple, but choosing different words to articulate what has happened and is still happening helps. Using words like 'survivor' over 'victim' or 'experienced' over 'suffered' doesn't diminish the impact of dreadful events, but rather, it gives me a sense that I can recover and move forward. At times, when something has become too complicated, I re-phrase it, and instead of saying, 'I can't do that,' I'll say, 'I *can* do this instead.' These are small changes, but changes repeated daily can help alter negative thinking. Since I've acquired the mobility scooter, it has, to some extent, replaced the freedom taken away by being unable to drive. I was fearful at first, but I started small; I just drove a few metres to get used to it and then turned around. Then, driving down the lane, then on the footpath and finally to the park.

I still do word challenges and crosswords to keep my brain alive.

I buy *Take 5* and *That's Life* magazines every week and do the games religiously.

I've been watching Ninja Warrior lately. Being a former gymnast, I know I could have done those challenges and done them well. I get irritated watching it, but I can't stop watching. I understand how those people train. I know how fit they are, and the discipline needed to get to that fitness level. It makes me want to jump into the television and have a go. I find myself moving and bursting to get up and participate with the challengers, but I can barely move to pick up the remote! I find myself screaming at the challengers, egging them on. I then yell at Jack. He's often with me. His comments on certain people drive me crazy.

"She's not going to make it. She jumped too early!" he'll say.

"Piss off! At least she's having a go!" I tell him as I bite into my chocolate cannoli.

Because I know what's involved in gymnastic moves, and I'm dying to do the same and can't, I'm sensitive to the efforts of the people doing what I once could have done. I then berate Jack, explaining to him about leanness and muscle mass and why that girl, even though she is short, didn't make the jump, not because of her shortness but because she didn't bounce high enough or long enough to generate the energy to push her body up to grab that rope or tyre or whatever she had to grab onto. It brings back memories of my days of peak fitness, and at times, I know I shouldn't watch it as it triggers something inside of me, a terrible ache for the life I once had. At times, I feel the will to get up off the lounge and try to jump. My head says yes, but my body will not obey.

Every Wednesday, I go to rehabilitation, and every week, it's getting harder. Some part of my body starts saying 'no' to me every week. This year, I decided to get household help with some things that are becoming difficult. I don't want to spend half a day making the bed anymore. It takes up too much time that could be spent doing other things that bring small slices of happiness into my day. I know some people would ask why I would even bother making the bed, but I like to feel organised. It helps me mentally. I have had to let go of thinking I can do without help. I'm glad it's there. I still believe that environmental medicine has helped me, and I encourage everyone to find a doctor who thinks outside the square and to find a counsellor they can trust. These days, I don't think about suicide. *I know I'm worth something.* I've worked out why I had such low self-esteem and what to do about it. I am not critical of anyone who is contemplating suicide or who has succeeded in ending their lives. I respect people's decisions, and I understand that sometimes the pain is too much to bear. I won't give in to suicide, but I would consider euthanasia. To me, they are different things. I don't want to end my life because I'm so depressed that I can't go on. I want to end it when I'm not depressed and can make a rational decision about what and how.

I'm not afraid to die. I was raised a Catholic, but I've moved away from traditional Catholicism. I consider myself more of a spiritual person than a Catholic. I believe there is a Heaven. After I had that experience on the operating table, I have absolutely no doubts. Over the past couple of years, I've read countless books on spirituality, death and dying the afterlife, Buddhist stuff, Christian stuff, non-religious stuff, self-help stuff and other stuff. Some of it has helped me, but, in the end, I think it is a person's own processing that leads them to acceptance of death. It is only recently that I've genuinely come to terms with my illness and how it has changed my life. This year, I've survived cancer, so I know I'm not ready to go – *just yet*.

I'm proud of myself for getting this all out and having the courage to talk about things in my private life that many people wouldn't want the world to know.

I don't know why my life turned out as it has, but I believe we're put here for a purpose, and perhaps mine is helping others who are in the same situation as I am or those who contemplate or act on a suicide wish like I once did. I have always thought I was here for a purpose, but I could never figure out exactly what it was. Sometimes, when I'm in one of those moods when I think this life is hell, I look at the beautiful things around me. When I look at dogs, I see that animals are unique, and then I think that this life can't be hell when there are so many beautiful things here on earth. There are still times when I ask myself why I keep going. In some ways, it's like the way I refuse to give in to the disease. This disease has taken everything from me. My career, my chance of meeting someone, my dreams of having children, of owning my own home, of being healthy and happy. Everything.

These days, I'm refusing to give in to suicide. It has taken years of therapy to realise that I'm a worthwhile person and that I don't deserve pain. Of course, I get down, but there are people to help me, friends, a team of professionals, and my dog!

I got my determination from my father. He taught me never to leave a job unfinished. When I was growing up, Mum would call us children to dinner, and sometimes I yelled out that I would be there as soon as I'd finished my homework or whatever I was doing. My mother would tell me that whatever it was could wait. My father would ask me to finish it first and then come down to dinner. I want to leave this earth with things finished, and for me, that means others knowing my life story in the hope that it may help someone else.

I am unwilling to give up. I could simply give in and do nothing, eat whatever I want, not exercise, leave rehab, and let my depression take over. Chronic depression, even with the proper medication, is still hard, but my answer to all that is no, I'm not giving in. I have always been a fighter. A girlfriend's partner calls me 'Trooper'. I'm not advocating a Pollyanna approach to life; my life is complicated, but the small, beautiful moments keep me going. I've always read, especially biographies and autobiographies, and I have been very fortunate to meet someone who taught me how to turn my story into a manuscript. It has given me a reason to keep going. It has been extremely therapeutic, as well. If my story encourages just one person not to commit suicide or to go into counselling and get the right help or to develop strategies to cope with a terminal illness, then I will have achieved something.

I'm donating my organs as I want to help someone who needs them. I'm having a cardboard coffin because they're better for the environment. Some friends of mine own a farm, and I've made arrangements with them to scatter my ashes over the land. I want them to be scattered in two places, one near the horses. I've been thinking about a brightly painted coffin with stars and M&Ms all over it. Recently, I heard about a company that fires people's ashes into the stars with a cannon. The ashes then release like fireworks. That idea appeals to me as well. What a way to go!

I am so grateful to my fantastic team: My amazing carer Caroline; my practitioners Christine Kipps, James Southern, Elizabeth Scott, Genevieve Woodbridge, Professor Bruce Brew (Teapot), Dr Steven Tisch, The Genetic Team at St Vincent's Hospital, Sydney, Dr Patel (Uncle Bug), Dr Neevan Somia, Dr Clare Fraser, Dr Lyn Cheim, Dr Sue McCully, Paul Dardagan and the team at Bounce Rehab Pyrmont.

I have wonderful friends, and I'd like to acknowledge them here: Jack, Dart, Mumski and my bubbies, Chip and Bow (Nicolette and Isabella), Jack & Elle,

Ughboot, Glenn, Wendy and Greg and the kids (Benjamin and Elizabeth) Tarny & Rob and Bayley, Jean Taylor and Jet, Postie Paul, Sophia, Dom Raf and Sassy, Angela, Jeff, Annika and Claudia, Jax's and Natalia, Jo and Frank Tuscano. You guys are my family.

    I'm saying goodbye to all the people who have hurt me. My mother and my sisters, my ex-husband, the men who assaulted me, the people who have taken advantage of me when I haven't been well enough to stand up for myself. I'm letting it all go. I have questions that I will never know the answers to. I don't talk to my disease anymore. I've accepted it. Having a conversation with my illness for all those years was the right thing for me to do. It kept me fighting and alive. It fostered a determination in me to plough through and keep going. Every day is precious, and I don't want to waste time thinking about people who aren't worth it. When you don't know how much time you have left, there is a definite shift in how you use that time. It teaches you to live in the present. It teaches you to let go of everything that has ever hurt you. It teaches you that there is much to do with the time we have left.

    This is the time of my life.

I would like to thank Melissa for our years of friendship and for trusting me to write her story, a task that saw us laugh, cry and eat many milk buns together.

I would like to thank my wonderful agent and editor, Irina Dunn for her editing work on the manuscript and finding us New Holland Publishers.

Jo Tuscano